Grateful to Have Been There

Bill W. and Nell Wing, New York City, during AA Conference Week, 1960s.

Grateful to Have Been There

My Forty-two Years with Bill and Lois, and the Evolution of Alcoholics Anonymous

Second Edition
(Expanded and Revised)

NELL WING

Hazelden Publishing

Hazelden Publishing
Center City, Minnesota 55012-0176
hazelden.org/bookstore

© 1992, 1998 by Hazelden Foundation
All rights reserved.
First published by Parkside Publishing Corporation, 1992
Second edition published by Hazelden 1998
Printed in the United States of America
No portion of this publication may be reproduced in any
manner without the written permission of the publisher.

Book design by Will H. Powers
Typesetting by Stanton Publication Services, Inc.
Cover design by David Spohn
All photos courtesy of the Hazelden-Pittman Archives

In memory of
Bill and Lois W.,
with love and gratitude for their
long and cherished friendship

Contents

CONTENTS

Acknowledgments

I wish to express grateful thanks to the following for their help and support and for allowing me access to materials pertaining to AA history with permission to reprint from them:

In particular, I am grateful for the help of the AA archives at the General Service Office (G.S.O.), the archivist, and AA World Services, Inc., for allowing me access to books, pamphlets, letters, and magazines. I also value deeply the sharing of personal memories by my friends who were employees of AA.

I am grateful to the AA Grapevine, Inc. for sharing source information and permission to reprint.

I extend special thanks to Al-Anon Family Group Headquarters, Inc., for their cooperation in reviewing material pertaining to Lois W. and for permission to use portions of it.

I wish to express special thanks to Mrs. Lucille Kahn for sharing her memories of meetings among Bill W., Gerald Heard, and Aldous Huxley, at her and her husband's apartment in New York City.

I am grateful for the help and guidance of Bob P. in collating and preparing the original materials.

Thanks to so many of my long-time AA friends, who so graciously shared their memories of Bill and Lois with me.

Nell Wing, 1962, at AA headquarters, New York City.

Preface

Nell Wing was executive secretary and assistant to Bill W., a co-founder of Alcoholics Anonymous, for seventeen years and was a close friend and long-time companion to Lois W., co-founder of Al-Anon, for thirty-four years. "They were my family," declares Nell, and indeed, no other individual has ever approached the warm and caring relationship she enjoyed with two of the most extraordinary figures of our time. Additionally, she worked at the World Services Office (w.s.o.) of AA from the beginning of 1947 until her retirement at the close of 1982, starting as receptionist and later becoming secretary to the AA World Services, Inc. She was a board researcher; publications editor; layout and production coordinator of the G.S.O. newsletters and Conference Report for several years; and finally archivist for the fellowship for the last ten of her years, during which several AA areas in the United States and Canada invited her to talk and share memories and anecdotes of her years with AA. No other living person knows more about how Alcoholics Anonymous developed and grew, no other living person has been as close and perceptive an observer of the excitement, turbulence, and spiritual underpinnings of what

Aldous Huxley called "the most important social movement of the Twentieth Century."

Over the years, Bill and Lois on numerous occasions inscribed messages of appreciation and affection to this close friend in letters and books. One of the last such expressions is inscribed in "The AA Way of Life," later renamed *As Bill Sees It.* "Lois joins me in deepest love and our endless gratitude for all that you have long given of yourself to us—and to AA's everywhere—In devotion, Bill." July 1967

In the flyleaf of AA publications that Bill W. presented
to his aide and assistant, Nell Wing, over the years, he
inscribed:

October 8, 1954
In deep appreciation of your wonderful and
long devotion to AA. And to me.

September 1957
. . . for your precious friendship and for
your devotion which helped so much to make this book
AA Comes of Age what it is.

July 1965
The thought that Providence has let you and me share
AA's Thirtieth Anniversary together stirs me
very greatly. Thanks be that you are so much
to so many—and to me.

1967
Lois joins me in deepest love and our endless
gratitude for all that you have in devotion long given
of yourself to us—and to AA's everywhere.

Grateful to Have Been There

1

Miami, January 1971

WE WERE ABOARD A LEAR JET chartered to take Bill W. from his home in Bedford Hills, New York, to the Miami Heart Institute in Miami, Florida. It was January 24, 1971. As the pilots maneuvered to the heights and speed necessary to get down there as quickly as possible without endangering Bill's fragile condition, Bill, now seriously ill, was lying on a stretcher laid across the backs of several seats, wearing his ever-present oxygen mask. Dr. Ed B., his physician, had placed Lois at Bill's head, where her physical presence and her own special love would aid him most. Ed sat at the patient's side, and I was seated near his feet.

As we flew, Bill slipped in and out of hallucinations, seeing dead or absent relatives at his feet, whom he would describe in detail for us. His left arm would occasionally slip off the narrow stretcher and hang down. I would lift it back onto his lap and give him a pat. He would try to smile and give my hand a grateful squeeze. I said simply, "Hold fast"—one of his own favorite expressions—"Hold fast, Bill."

That wasn't the first time the four of us had been in Miami in those last fateful months. The previous July we had all been

3

together at the International Convention of AA and Al-Anon—the largest gathering of the two fellowships ever held up to that time. It had been held at the Fountainbleu and Eden Roc hotels on Miami Beach. Over ten thousand members and their families had come from all over the world, expecting to see the cofounder and hear him speak, as he had at all four previous anniversary conventions.

But this time Bill was much too sick. His lifelong cigarette habit had caught up with him in the form of emphysema, which had been steadily progressing since 1965, even after Bill had given up smoking in 1969. In early spring of that year, while working up on the roof of his studio at Stepping Stones, Bill and Lois's home, he had almost fallen off, saved by a tree branch that broke the fall, but not entirely. Stubbornly, he returned to the roof to finish the job after resting and feeling for broken bones (there seemed to be none); but that was the beginning of the end. He never fully recovered from the effects of the fall, and his health began to deteriorate more rapidly. The following April, at AA's annual General Service Conference dinner, he was unable to finish his opening talk, to the shock and consternation of the delegates, trustees, and all present.

In July, I had flown down with Bill and Lois to the Miami convention a few days early. At these gatherings, I stayed pretty much at Bill's side to do his errands, help with his notes for his talks, attempt to protect him from the crowds, who always pressed in on him, and generally help out. This time, it was clear that Bill wasn't up to his scheduled appearances. The usual press conference was held the Wednesday afternoon before the weekend conference began. Dr. Jack Norris substituted for Bill, I remember, and Lois was present, of course—a difficult time for her.

Every day, once or sometimes twice a day, we had to take Bill back and forth to the clinic. Lois, Bob H. (general manager of AA's General Service Office), and Dr. Jack were all stretched out and spread pretty thin trying to cope—trying to keep the huge convention going on schedule and improvising excuses for Bill's failure to appear. I spent most of the daytime with Bill in his and Lois's suite upstairs at the hotel, taking messages, checking on his needs, running errands, and so forth—actually he slept most of the time. It was during that week, starting on the trip down, that he began hallucinating; for example, he imagined he had made a long-distance call. It was all terribly distressing to Lois, but she managed heroically, fulfilling her Al-Anon appearances and some of Bill's, guiding and comforting all of us. If anyone could rise to any occasion, it was Lois W.!

Bernard Smith, the past chair of the General Service Board and a good friend of Bill's, was called down from New York to deliver the main talk that Saturday night in Bill's place. Bern appeared a little disgruntled at the short notice and asked me to help him adapt a conference talk of his from previous years—which we did. I recall we finished up Saturday about one or two o'clock in the afternoon, whereupon he left to play a little golf. On Sunday, when I saw him in the hotel lobby, he came over to apologize for his irritability the day before. Taking my arm, he said, "Come along, Nell, I'll buy you a drink," and we moved into the Fountainbleu bar, ordered drinks, and reminisced a bit about the old days. (Ironically, Bern Smith died suddenly only three weeks later, on August 1, less than six months before Bill.)

I was so exhausted by Saturday night, after the tiring session with Bern and worrying about events of the past few days, that I had slept in on Sunday morning—and thereby missed Bill's last public appearance!

During the huge closing meeting that morning, Bill put in an unannounced, surprise appearance. I'm told they wheeled him in from the back of the stage, hooked up with tubes to an oxygen tank and clad, at his own insistence, in one of the garish orange blazers that identified the Miami host committee! I understand the whole hall simply exploded into applause, the people cheering as tears of joy rolled down their cheeks. As the noise subsided, he heaved himself up from the wheelchair to his full height, hands on the rostrum. He spoke for perhaps only five minutes, his voice clear and strong, the old Bill at his best. He spoke of how impressed he was with the large attendance, particularly of members from countries abroad. He mentioned what it had meant to him to see AA's enormous growth and to have been a part of it. And he ended with a few moving words that the thousands who heard them will never forget, saying, in effect, "As I look out this morning on this vast crowd, I know in my heart that Alcoholics Anonymous will surely last a thousand years—if it is God's will!" As he sat down in his wheelchair, the audience rose in a tumultuous standing ovation.

Later that day, I flew back to New York. Bill returned to Miami Heart Institute with Lois, where Dr. Ed could better supervise his worsening condition. They remained in Miami until the first of August, when the decision was made to return home to Stepping Stones. Hardly had they done so when Bill's condition took another downturn. His illness started to progress rapidly. He began to require oxygen during the day; later at night also. His hallucinations were coming more frequently.

Bill first had a male nurse; in a couple of months, another aide was added so he was attended around the clock. During this time, I was coming up to Stepping Stones more often, marveling at Lois's incredible courage and energy. In mid-January, my own mother died, and I had just returned a few days prior to the climactic events of that last weekend at Stepping Stones.

Early in the evening on Saturday, January 23, Lois and I

were seated in the large library room outside their bedroom upstairs. Bill suddenly called out from the bedroom for a drink of water. The day aide had finished his duty. The night aide, due at nine o'clock, had not arrived. Thinking of being some help to Lois, I fetched him a glass, helped him sit up a bit, and cradled his head so he could drink it. Swallowing too quickly, he choked, started deep coughing, couldn't get his breath. I thought, "My God, we'll lose him right here!" But just then, miraculously, a car raced up the driveway and the aide rushed in! Sensing he would be needed, he said, he had decided to come in early. He used the correct procedure to help Bill's choking spasms and so settled him down for the rest of the night. I still marvel at this incredible coincidence, if that is the right word.

Midmorning on Sunday, January 24, an ambulance was called, and we were all taken to the Westchester airport in White Plains in the early afternoon to await the Lear jet Brinkley Smithers, an old friend of Bill's, had ordered. It was to take us to the Miami Heart Institute. The plane wasn't there yet, however, nor did it arrive for what seemed an eternity as we waited anxiously by the passenger gate. Bill was in the ambulance, requiring constant attention by the aides. Lois, now frantic at the delay, dashed out upon the small runway area of the airport, searching the sky for a sign of the plane. Soon they had to order her off the field. Just as the aides were about to take Bill back to the Westchester hospital, the jet finally arrived with Dr. Ed! We boarded and took off.

In Miami, we were met by AAs and driven to the Miami Heart Institute, where we left Bill. Lois and I checked into separate rooms side by side, at a nearby motel, had a bite to eat, and finally fell into our beds. The phone awaked me at 12:30 A.M. It was Dr. Ed, in the lobby, telling me Bill was dead and wondering whether to awaken Lois. Bill had died at 11:30 P.M.,

January 24, 1971—on the fifty-third anniversary of his and Lois's wedding. AA had lost its cofounder, Lois had lost her beloved husband, and I had lost my closest friend and confidant, the big brother/father figure of my later life. The death certificate noted he had endured emphysema for three years and pneumonia for two weeks. Congestive heart failure was also named among the contributing causes of death. On the flight down Ed had pointed out the presence of the congestive heart failure.

Before awakening me, Ed had already called Bob H. in New York, which set into action a preplanned procedure for notifying everyone who needed to know, both in and out of Alcoholics Anonymous. When Dr. Ed and the other AA couples came to my room, we stayed up talking the rest of the night, debating every few minutes whether to waken Lois and tell her—but deciding each time to let her sleep a little while more, knowing she was exhausted and anticipating more to come. This night, there was no stirring. No apparent break in her sound sleep, which we had anticipated using as the opportunity to call her and break the news. It was probably nearly 7:00 A.M. when we heard her stirring in the next room. Ed broke the news to her, and she collapsed into his arms, utterly devastated. She remained hurt and angry to the end of her life that the hospital hadn't notified her immediately of the turn for the worse so she could have been with Bill, and also perturbed because we hadn't told her immediately of his passing.

Bill had always loved his home state of Vermont and had planned to be buried there with the rest of his family. So it was decided to keep his body in cold storage in Miami—in a Vermont oak casket, which Ed arranged for—until the New England earth thawed sufficiently for the interment. This took place on May 8 in East Dorset, Vermont, with a small family group of us present.

I flew back from Miami with Lois on Monday. Through her grief and tears, she murmured more to herself than to me, "I was too possessive." The demands of Bill's AA work and the office had taken him away from her at least a couple of days a week, and she had always been understandably jealous of this.

The next day, the *New York Times* ran a front-page obituary with a picture of Bill, recounting the main points of his life and contributions to AA. Hundreds of other newspapers around the world also carried obituaries (filling three special scrapbooks in the AA archives today.) The world knew for the first time the identity of the man who had cofounded Alcoholics Anonymous. (Dr. Bob's identity had also been revealed when he died in November 1950, so the precedent had already been set.) On February 14, St. Valentine's Day, simultaneous memorial services were held worldwide, from the cathedral of St. John the Divine in New York to Montreal, London, Antwerp, Bombay, Dublin, Glasgow, Johannesburg, Melbourne, and Istanbul. Also, memorials were held all over the United States and Central and South America. At Stepping Stones the preceding week, we had held a family service. A close friend, the local Congregational minister, presided and I played the piano, stumbling badly over one of the hymns.

Though we had lost Bill, for me this was actually the beginning of a long, closer companionship with Lois, which lasted until her death seventeen years later. I continued my every-other-weekend visits to Stepping Stones, not only to help comfort her initially, but to extend my loving friendship, to share many projects we planned, to enjoy our favorite games, and to accompany her on several travels. Our relationship blossomed into a mutual love and companionship that I will continue to cherish all my life.

Meanwhile, I continued my work and projects at the General Service Office. I was occupied at first in cleaning out the office Bill and I had shared and then tending to his posthumous affairs and correspondence, and organizing his papers, talks, and files. Along with collecting group and intergroup histories, G.S.O. matters, and General Service Conferences, these categories evolved naturally into the basic framework for the archives.

2

How I Came to Work for AA

*M*Y BEGINNINGS WERE IN West Kendall, a small town located in upstate New York, near the shores of Lake Ontario. My father, Frank Wing, was a schoolteacher and one of the two local justices of the peace. Dad was a stern disciplinarian as a schoolteacher. When he wore another hat as a local judge, however, he seemed to be considerate and understanding of all sorts of problems, including drinking. Local rumor had it that my father indulged in a beer or two occasionally, but said rumor never reached the ears of our mother, who was firmly addicted to the Women's Christian Temperance Union (WCTU)! It's my interpretation that Dad, while perhaps not thinking of alcoholism in the exact terms of an illness or disease at that time, nonetheless did view excessive drinking as more complicated than just a moral problem. (That not a few of those arrested were Dad's friends might have been a leavening factor in his tolerance.) I think most of the drunk arrests were for drunk driving—in the middle of the night. This was when we would all be awakened by the pounding on the door by the state troopers, with their swaying victims in hand. Dad often paid the fines of his friends, for of course they seldom had any cash left by that time. In any case, had there been an AA group in our area in those days, as there is today, I'm sure Dad would have sentenced the steady repeaters to "AA or thirty days."

My mother, becoming better informed about AA as time went on (my father died in 1945, two years before I came to the Alcoholic Foundation—later AA) and listening to my oft-repeated stories and descriptions of AA, became a staunch fan of the fellowship. When Bill and Lois visited her one summer when they were in the area, she became even more addicted, with lots of enthusiasm, bringing to the meetings of the WCTU up-to-date news of the fellowship, or anecdotes about Bill and Lois, unaware of or disregarding the frowns and stares of the Temperance ladies who weren't all that devoted to AA and its program!

I remember that the WCTU headquarters, in early 1952, messed up as far as AA was concerned: Appearing in their newsletter was the statement that Bill W had had a slip and gone back to drinking—obviously, no attempt at verification had been made. But we didn't let it "slip" by. Bill, on AA headquarters stationery, addressed a strongly worded letter to the editor, stating that her information was erroneous and that he expected to see the error corrected in the next issue. Indeed it was, with apology.

I remember, also, that the WCTU made overtures to gain our cooperation in their prevention campaigns in those earlier years, as did liquor companies, to no avail of course. In fact, about a hundred years earlier, the liquor industry had sought and obtained the cooperation of some alcoholics in the Washington movement in speaking for them about the need for moderation in drinking.

In the fall of 1936, I attended Keuka College, located in New York's Finger Lakes region. During my four years there, it was an all-girls' school, later to become coed. But we dated boys from nearby colleges and held frequent dinners and dances, where dates could be invited. I guess I would describe myself in those days as a kind of prehippie type—many years ahead of their time! I think this was because we were a bit ahead of other schools—maybe more self-assured. We were encouraged to express ourselves in many areas, to make our own decisions; we had more freedom of choice to select subjects to major in. We invited well-known people—from many levels of society—to speak at our assembly meetings. I remember Eleanor Roosevelt especially, for her wise counsel and sharing with us, as she sat in the middle of the room after her talk. We all sat on the floor around her, asking questions.

I remember to this day her advice concerning maturity: Don't expect everyone you meet to like or appreciate you, your ideas, or even your person: Accept and "know thyself," and be yourself. I was agnostic yet idealistic, pretty much centered on self, nonconformist but searching, testing every "pie counter" as Bill used to say in describing his own search for faith. But I think this describes every person at that age.

Upon graduation in 1940, with my BA degree in education, I journeyed down to my mother's hometown of San Antonio, Texas, the next year. There I taught in a high school for Mexican children. They were ragamuffins, lovable but difficult to discipline. Some of them carried knives and enjoyed exercising a little mayhem on opposing football teams if they lost the game. I spoke a little Spanish learned in college and from Dad (who had lived in Mexico at one time and for a while in Texas, where he met and married Daisy Shapard, my mother). Anyway, I think the kids enjoyed "Mees Weeng."

Before the year was up, however, I had had just about all I could take of teaching, including a bad case of ringworm, caught apparently from one of my pupils. I turned to secretarial work at the San Antonio Arsenal. (It was World War II time.)

After another year I returned home, as Dad had suffered a heart attack. He recovered and lived another three years, but I stayed on in Rochester, taking another secretarial job.

One day, two girls in my office decided to go over to the Coast Guard Auxiliary recruiting station during lunch hour and urged me to go along with them. Once there, I was persuaded to take the physical and qualifying tests too. As it turned out, neither of my friends passed the tests—but I did! So I joined the female arm of the Coast Guard, the SPARS, which stood for Semper Paratus Always Ready. This, as you can imagine, titillated our navy and coast guard dates no end. I was stationed in the Seattle Thirteenth Naval District for about two years and enjoyed my duty there. I did not particularly enjoy, at one point, being "awarded" a Captain's Mast (lowest stage of navy court martial) for an all-night drinking spree. This came from doing it at the wrong time, in the wrong place, in the wrong company, an episode I was to recall, what I could remember of it, in later years.

I was discharged as boatswain's mate, second class, at the end of the war. I was not involved in any serious relationship but deeply interested in sculpture, for which I had some talent. I had a strong desire but only a vague plan to head for Mexico to study under a famous sculptor who taught at the American University, at that time located near San Miguel de Allende, a beautiful area above Mexico City with a large international community. I thought it would be lots of fun to settle in with those people and their intriguing lifestyle. Yet I was being practical, too, since I would be starting a career.

But first I needed some money to supplement my small severance pay from the service. So I came down to New York City. I was at an employment agency, seeking a temporary job. The interviewer studied my résumé, then came over to the table, leaned across, and whispered—as if the walls had ears—"How would you like to work at Alcoholics Anonymous?"

As it happened, I knew a little about AA. For some reason, I've retained all these years a clear memory of sitting on my bed at college, in late September 1939, reading that wonderful article in *Liberty* magazine, entitled "Alcoholics and God," by Morris Markey. AA was described favorably, but religion was emphasized—so I wasn't too optimistic about its future. Still in my agnostic phase, the emphasis on a questionable deity (to my way of thinking) was a fatal mistake. So much for my accuracy as a prophet. Over the next few years, I read more articles on AA in the *Saturday Evening Post, Reader's Digest,* and other magazines. I was intrigued by all of them. So, at the employment agency, I didn't need to think about it. I replied enthusiastically that I would love to try the job, whatever it was.

Thus it was that on the cold, blustery morning of Monday, March 3, 1947, I showed up at the AA office (called the Alcoholic Foundation) at 415 Lexington Avenue, just across from Grand Central Station. (Alas, "415 Lex" is no more; there is now a huge, modern, glitzy, block-filled building, called 425 Lexington Avenue.) The office was located on the eleventh floor, three small rooms, with a complement of about a dozen people, including two AA staff members (who were called "secretaries" then). I was met at the door by Charlotte L., who was quite new herself (six months), and taken over to meet Marian Weaver, the new office manager, also recently engaged (two months).

After we had chatted, mostly about our service experiences Marian—recently discharged from the WAVES (navy)—told me quite seriously that the salary would be small but that the spiritual rewards of working there, the satisfaction of helping people, would be great. That appealed to my idealism, and I readily admitted I could use a little spiritual input myself—not to be overdone, of course. But not until my first paycheck did I realize how truly small the salary would be, nor until later how great the spiritual rewards. Anyway, I started to work the next day. Alcoholics Anonymous was not quite twelve years old; I was twenty-nine.

The next day, Tuesday, Bill W. appeared in the office. His usual pattern was to spend one or two days a week there, then and almost to the end of his life. Again, it was Charlotte who took me in to meet him, saying, "And this is Bill." Then she left us. Holding out my hand, I expected the usual polite amenities, but I'm not sure he even said hello.

I do remember that he eased his long, lanky frame into a straight-backed chair, bending way over backward on its two rear legs, his hands in his pockets, glasses on top of his head, and immediately launched into a long, rather irritated monologue, complaining about how the trustees were trying to keep him isolated from the membership and just wanted him to stay in a kind of "ivory tower" and concentrate on writing projects. Also, he went on about a need for something called a General Service Conference, composed of members from all across the country to come to New York and take responsibility for future decision making for the fellowship. Since I didn't have the vaguest idea of what he was talking about, I confess I escaped as soon as I decently could.

But right then and there I learned at least two important characteristics about Bill W.: One, he was not much given to small talk, and two, he possessed a good measure of "tunnel vision." This meant he could become totally absorbed with his thoughts, ideas, and visions for AA and its future. So, what often appeared to be absentmindedness was really inner preoccupation with problems and decisions that later evolved over the next decade into the movement's structural and service framework.

In fact, he was not really an attentive listener unless you asked a question or spoke about a subject he was especially interested in; in that case, it could be difficult to get away. Later on, when Bill and I shared a large room at 305 East Forty-Fifth Street, I watched visitors who just wanted to poke their heads in to say hello get caught up in one of Bill's discourses. Soon they felt unable to say they had to leave and I had the feeling, as they sometimes glanced furtively at their watches, that they were in danger of missing or had already missed their plane, train, or maybe even boat. But I want to emphasize at the same time that Bill was always ready to listen to any of us if we wanted advice or an opinion on a subject he felt he could share—he was always there for us.

Nell Wing served in 1945–1946 in the female arm of the Coast Guard, the SPARS (Semper Paratus Always Ready).

17

3

Getting to Know You

A ONE-WORD IMPRESSION of that first week in our small AA office was *disarray*. Counting Bill and now myself, there were about thirteen people crowded into three small rooms—the walls of which were frequently moved, or pulled down and put up again to achieve as much space as possible as new people were added to the work force. In a casual and permissive way, the nonalcoholic employees appeared to have divided up the office jobs to suit themselves, prior to the recent hiring of the new office manager, Marian Weaver. (Bill spent about two days a week at the office, coming down by train from his and Lois's home in Bedford Hills.)

There were two AA staff members. The senior one was Margaret (Bobbie) B., who I was told had been a nightclub dancer in Paris in the 1920s. In the fashion of the forties, she wore tiny little box hats at work and went tripping along on high heels. But she was a terrific communicator. I can't tell you the number of alcoholics—all over the AA world—who owe their sobriety to that special lady. Office discipline, however, did not appear to be her long suit. She did attempt one enforcement—a rule that she was to be called "Mrs. B——," and Bill, "Mr. W——." (Come to think of it, I don't remember that we were supposed to give the same courtesy to Charlotte.)

During the 1947 fall New York Intergroup dinner, when the office was chockablock with visitors, mostly from out of state, I was at my desk near the switchboard. A call came in for Bill, and observing our new rule, I called out, "There's a call for you, Mr. W———." To which Bill, moving over to take the call, spoke up loudly, "Hey, what the hell, Nell, are you still calling me 'Mr. W———'?" It was very embarrassing. I thought, my gosh, what will people think? In any case, this effort at big-office formality didn't last long and has never been tried since.

The second staff member, Charlotte, on the other hand, was a good businesswoman. She lent stability and a lot of practical know-how to the whole office operation. From the advertising agency where they both had worked, Charlotte had brought in Marian Weaver to be office manager. When Marian proceeded to introduce some needed office reform and discipline, most of the employees quit or were let go. I was the first of the "new breed."

Even so, while Marian was inaugurating the new procedures, it was still sometimes like a scene from "You Can't Take It with You." Mary Lou, our clerk typist, was a bit of a merry madcap and our office "princess"—there's generally one in every office. She was a happy, good-natured girl who liked to tease. I remember her marching around the office, sporting a paper bag over her head. We all enjoyed her antics and the visitors did also. The shipping clerk had a crush on her, sitting at her desk a good part of the time, feet up, comfortably leaning back in his chair, while I or whoever was available did the packing and handling of the literature pickups for visitors in my reception area. I think Mary Lou was the last employee of the "old era" to leave. We missed her.

The informality among the staff when I first arrived extended to some of the "visitors." Though the New York Inter-group had been in operation for a year or more, the local active alcoholics who knew about A A or who were in and out of the fellowship, or who learned quickly anyway, soon discovered we might be a good source for a handout, and they often looked us up. They lounged in the reception room to sleep or pass out until quite firmly shown the door and the elevator.

One day, in the reception room (I saw a lot of the "passing parade," as you can imagine), a guy went into D. T. 's. He began gesturing and screaming about a big snake under his chair. To this, the employees in the back room (clerks, typists, etc.) responded rapidly by rushing for the elevators. That part of the office emptied quickly. On being called back before the elevators arrived, they filed sheepishly in to their desks. But there was no heavy-handed or angry dismissal of these fellows. Though we had been told not to give them any money, we did sneak a few coins into their hands occasionally. Hank G. (an early general manager) or Bill or whoever assisted in the exit, was caring and tried to instill the notion that the men could return if and when they wanted to get sober.

Those wonderful A A staff members Bobbie and Charlotte, and a few months later Ann M. and Susan (who for a short period of time helped with correspondence) carried an enormous workload, compounded by the rearrangements and adjustments in the office. Also in this period of the later forties, the groups were proliferating at a fast pace in the United States and Canada. Groups in prisons and hospitals (especially V A hospitals) were coming along and growing steadily. The staff had to handle all this and deal with the increasing publicity A A was receiving. So they worked long hours all week and then, as now, went out to speak and attend local A A or weekend gatherings in various parts of the United States and Canada.

I was initially hired to be secretary to Charlotte but was soon put to work as receptionist switchboard operator also. After the exodus of the employees who were there when I came, the next group hired were more experienced and disciplined. Some had alcoholic relatives, and a couple had alcoholic problems themselves. And the rest of us, as Bill said, "thought alcoholically anyway," so we all fit together wonderfully. Within a week or two of coming to the office, I realized that it was going to take a little longer to get to Mexico than I had anticipated.

Soon, in fact, I began to feel that all of us related like a family. That feeling was encouraged, and Bill and others also impressed on us that we shared an opportunity and a responsibility to help the still-suffering alcoholic through our work and service, as Marian had suggested during our interview. We were encouraged to have a concerned attitude and a sympathetic understanding of AA's purpose, principles, and goals. And I'm happy to say that the same feeling prevails to a remarkable degree even today, although the General Service Office is now much larger, with its one hundred–plus employees spread out over five full floors of the buildings at 468–470 Park Avenue South.

That decade 1945–55 was the most turbulent, exciting, and innovative era in the history of Alcoholics Anonymous. Bill was caught up in it too—we all were, in the office especially. As receptionist, I greeted everybody who came through the door, listened to local and personal problems when the staff got tied up, and then besides my other duties, started working with Bill in late 1950.

Although accurate membership record-keeping was almost impossible then (and still is!), we estimated there were about forty thousand members in 1947 and about 1,250 groups, with new groups forming at a rapid rate as the fellowship began to spread abroad. Several women's groups had begun by the early forties, for black members by the mid- to late forties, International Doctor's and International Seamen's groups in the late forties also. By the early fifties, groups were springing up for young people, lawyers (called "International Lawyers"), priests and nuns, gay people, and in later years airline pilots ("Birds of a Feather"). The message of AA was being carried by traveling salesman members and by vacationers as civilian travel resumed and people moved about after the war. Abroad, the message was carried by visitors from the United States and Canada, by loners, AA service personnel stationed abroad after the war, by merchant marine seamen, AA members in U.S. embassies, and construction workers on overseas jobs in Arab countries (I remember the excitement of our first Arab members!), where the need for AA help surfaced occasionally later on. It was exhilarating for us in the office to witness this acceleration of AA growth, already in Canada, Mexico, and Hawaii, to Ireland, Great Britain, Scotland, continental Europe, South Africa, Australia, Japan, Antarctica, Nepal (right on top of the world) and the Orient—and more—and to participate in service to those far-flung groups.

Those early members and new groups were often truly isolated. The loners had no one to communicate with except our office. We were their only contact and source for staying sober. So they wrote long letters, often from really distant and isolated places: deep in Africa, in U.S. bases in Greenland, and remote islands in the Atlantic and Pacific and Far East (Guam, Sumatra, etc.), describing how they felt, how they were doing, what luck they were having finding other alcoholics. Then came the letters, bursting with enthusiasm at finding another person or two and later, a letter saying "our group is having its first meeting tonight" and "thanks for your help." These letters, which so poignantly carry the story of how AA started and grew all over the world—these unique and precious communications, holding the history of AA forever safe and intact—I treasured deeply in our archives. There are also the stories of others I call "Johnny Appleseeds," members like Captain Jack S., who started the International Seamen's group; "Caracas Lil," who carried AA to so many places (living for some time in Venezuela); and Johnny P., and Irwin M., and Roy Y., who spread the message in various areas of the United States. Their letters are all retained in our AA archives at G.S.O.

As receptionist I was often the first one to learn from a visitor that a new group had been formed in his or her area. The first step would be to check the records to make sure we didn't have the group already listed. If we didn't, then we would get the information right there and then by taking the person to the "back room" to speak to our records clerk. After that we would make a little ceremony out of escorting the visitor over to a big U.S. map on the wall, where he or she would place a pin in the proper location. This was lots of fun for us all. Finally, I would take the visitor in to meet and chat with Bobbie, Charlotte, Ann, and later other staff members. All of this took about fifteen minutes. Today a tour of the five floors takes at least an hour. Sometimes that amount of time is spent just on the archives.

There had been many press stories on AA from the beginning of the forties (and even earlier), but newspapers, magazines, and radio seemed to "discover" AA in the middle forties. "Ask an Alcoholic" was a popular call-in radio program. Detroit and Hartford, Connecticut, had popular and creative radio documentaries on alcoholism and AA. Even regular radio programs, like early "soaps," carried the AA story lines. One such was called *Aunt Jenny,* popular in 1949, which devoted a ten-episode drama to a story of an alcoholic who found a way out in AA. This was broadcast over eighty-one stations of CBS. Over three hundred inquiries came into the Alcoholic Foundation before the series was finished. The AA *Grapevine* carried a good write-up of the program in its December 1949 issue, saying the subject was handled expertly and in an adult manner. Because we were all working during the day, of course, I don't remember if anyone had an opportunity to listen to these episodes. I know I didn't, but I do recall how excited we were at the publicity and good review of the series.

In later 1945, a movie, *The Lost Weekend*, had a terrific impact upon the public in that it portrayed the life of an alcoholic more realistically than had ever been done before, bringing to the general public an understanding of alcoholism as an illness. This movie was the major publicity turning point in helping AA to be understood, in carrying its message far and wide over the succeeding years.

As a result of this new perspective on alcoholism and interest in alcoholics, movie companies descended upon our small office, five or six in one year. We held lots of discussions—in the office, among trustees, and in communication with AA countrywide—on how much to cooperate, if at all. One contact with Hal Wallis of Paramount hung fire for about four years. A couple of scripts were offered, while the debate continued. The project finally petered out in 1949.

More than that, every day almost, AA was in the news, connected to some facet of publicity—there were magazine articles galore; the same with newspapers. Our clipping service poured in clippings. Our scrapbooks, begun in 1939, made interesting reading for visitors to the office, as they do today in the archives. AA was the subject frequently, though often facetiously, of comedians and cartoonists, many being members themselves. New books with AA themes—*September Remember* and *Breakdown*—were made into movies, both starring Susan Hayward, I think. Jim Bishop, well-known writer and reporter in that time, wrote most clearly and sympathetically about a well-known writer's alcoholism in a book called *The Glass Crutch.*

Another popular book was *If a Maid Be Mad,* by Harold Maine. (I remember reading this one especially. I think it was the first time I had read about an alcoholic's bouts with D.T.'s, described so wrenchingly, explicitly, and realistically. I've never forgotten the description of his terrifying episodes over all these years). The especially uplifting volume we all read that is still popular was *Modern Man in Search of a Soul,* by Dr. Carl Jung. I hurried to buy this book as soon as I could. (Meaning as soon as I had some money to spend. It did take a while.) *This Believing World,* by Lewis Browne, was a turning point in my own maturing and "search" for spirituality. I still love this book.

There were documentaries on AA by The March of Time and RKO Pathe. There were plays on Broadway: *Harvey* (about an alcoholic), *Come Back, Little Sheba,* and *The Cup of Trembling.* These also were made into movies. There were more movies and plays featuring AA in the fifties, and a good television movie, *One Day at a Time,* in 1955.

In AA itself, excellent local publications abounded—most with imaginative and pertinent titles, such as *The Eye Opener, The Sahara, The Stew, Hi and Dry, The Screwball* (I love that title), *The Thought Starter,* the AA *Grapevine,* of course, *The Boomerang,* and *The Paradox*—to name just a few!

By the late forties or early fifties, there were the beginnings of groups following the Twelve Steps: for example, Fatties Anonymous, Addicts Anonymous, Youth Anonymous, and Recovery, Inc. (Chicago–based) used principles similar to AA.

On the one hand, this rash of publicity created more demands on the staff responding to writers and reporters. On the other hand, it brought in more visitors for us to handle. And since the staff was often under pressure, there wasn't always enough time to do more than greet visitors. I did a lot of greeting and sharing of information and talking. I was particularly impressed with the number of nonalcoholics who stopped in the office to pick up a copy of the Twelve Steps, having been told about them or having read them somewhere. They wanted to use the Steps in their own life. That's when I first realized that the Twelve Steps are helpful to "outsiders," with almost any problem you can name—or as spiritual guidance.

I was also aware of the growing pains and problems that Alcoholics Anonymous was experiencing because the office was so frequently asked to help with solutions. Besides Bill and Dr. Bob, there were lots of local "founders" around the country. Since group (and personal) autonomy is an important tradition in the fellowship, many of these local founders spoke, acted, and gave guidance pretty much as they wanted. Also many of them were AA newsletter editors in their localities, and they had a wonderful opportunity to express and seek support for their own viewpoints. Many hung onto power and wouldn't always listen to newer members. Clubs for AAs were started, and they caused some confusion—what should be the purpose, how should they raise money, and so on. There were other problems—including some boy-girl problems and gambling raids. Money was a problem at both the group level and nationally. Bill and the first members recognized the importance of the principle of self-support. The greedy grasping for lots of money had been the downfall of some previous fellowships. Bill, learning from experience, vowed that would not happen to AA. John D. Rockefeller, Jr., expressed the same point of view, though probably not from the historical standpoint as did Bill and the other members.

The custom of holding area conferences and conventions started in the mid-forties. The big meeting in Cleveland in 1945 could almost be called an international convention.

Representatives from a couple foreign countries attended. The attendance was about twenty-five hundred. Also in the middle of the decade, intergroup offices opened up, bringing stability and information procedures to their areas.

Bill gave major talks during this decade before important medical societies, signifying growing awareness, interest, and approval by medical authorities of AA's contributions to the field. (Bill quoted a significant comment following his talk before the 1949 Montreal meeting of the American Psychiatric Association [APA]. One physician explained that the enthusiastic reception Bill received was due in large part to what he said, but also was an acknowledgment of failure on the part of medical people to cope with the problem.)

Mentioning Bill's appearances before medical societies reminds me of one of his close friends, Bunky, a scholar and biologist, more properly known and addressed as Dr. E. M. Jellinek, now deceased. One of the founders of the Yale Summer School of Alcohol Studies in 1943, he was also a methodical and dedicated researcher into the study of alcoholism during the 1940s and following decades and the author of the book *The Disease Concept of Alcoholism.*

In 1972, Lois and I had planned an exciting voyage via cruise ship to see the solar eclipse, which was to take place at a spot south of Nova Scotia and about a few hundred miles straight east from New York City into the Atlantic. At that point, God willing and the weather favorable, the sun and moon would merge and a thrilling experience would be ours. And it was indeed. But at Rutgers University, the Summer School of Alcohol Studies (formerly at Yale) was holding a dinner to commemorate the life and good works of Dr. Jellinek and to announce the first Jellinek Award—to Bill W., posthumously. Of course, this meant that Lois should be present to receive the award. Indeed, she did want to be present. So she decided to have it both ways. The dinner at Rutgers was to take place on the day we were to put in at Halifax. There Lois planned to disembark and take a plane to Rutgers, or rather New Brunswick. There was, however, no plane out of Halifax when we landed, and this was a disappointment to Lois and I'm sure to all those gathered at Rutgers.

Some time later, the award was delivered to Lois at Stepping Stones. It was a rather small bust of Jellinek, and there was no inscription on it, nothing at all, not his name nor who it was awarded to—nor who had awarded it. But it was a darling replication of the head and shoulders of that dear man. I'm absolutely sure both he and Bill had a good laugh about it up there as much as Lois and I did, because we loved to make a good story of it. (Oh yes, Lois had the statue sent out to be engraved with the important information—its resting place today is still up at the studio, where Bill worked.)

But to return to the problems of the forties. In 1946 Bill suddenly found himself in the middle of a dispute brought about by the National Council on Alcoholism or, as it was called early on, the National Council for Education on Alcoholism (NCEA) and a fund-raising project. This centered on a solicitation letter, prepared by Marty M. (that is, it carried her signature) that stated that Alcoholics Anonymous would benefit from any contributions received. Bill was on the spot because Marty was a personal friend, and he believed strongly in what she was trying to accomplish; hence, he had loyally and publicly endorsed her efforts, as well as her anonymity break. Indeed, both his and Dr. Bob's names appeared on the NCEA letterhead. When the solicitation letter involving AA was circulated, this brought a spate of outraged calls and letters into the office for such a long time, about four years, that I for one seriously thought it might be the end of the fellowship as we knew it. The trustees held their first public press conference ever, disclaiming any benefit to AA from NCEA contributions. Bill and Dr. Bob, acknowledging the necessity, withdrew from the NCEA, and their names were removed from its letterhead. However, some good came out of this incident. By 1949 it helped firmly establish the AA Traditions of nonaffiliation and self-support.

In the same way, the anonymity breaks that seemed to be occurring all the time helped shape the Eleventh and Twelfth Traditions. Marty M. had traveled around the country in the early forties promoting her organization, freely identifying herself publicly as an AA member. The furor that this caused—along with instances of other AA members "going public"—led Bill to rethink the overriding spiritual importance of anonymity, even his own, regardless of whatever temporary benefit might result from such a break. Or, as he put it, "the good is often the enemy of the best." Later on of course, true to these strong beliefs, Bill was to turn down public honors such as a cover story in *Time* magazine, an honorary doctorate from Yale, a couple of recommendations for a Nobel prize, a listing in *Who's Who,* and many others.

Ebby T., the man who brought the Oxford Group message to Bill, was a familiar visitor at 415 Lexington. Important as he was in the beginning of AA, he was never able to achieve any lasting sobriety himself. He dropped in at the office occasionally to cadge a little money from Bill—or anyone else he could put the touch on. When he was sober, I found him fun to talk to sitting in the reception area where I was. He was intelligent and articulate. Besides, he knew about some Wing families in the Albany area, where his own roots were.

One day when I was at my reception desk, Ebby came in very drunk. He wobbled and mumbled around the area for a while and then passed out over on the couch, where I left him. After a while the office door opened and a well-dressed, rather "British"-appearing stranger walked in. He explained to me that he was writing an article on AA history and that he knew enough about Bill W. and Dr. Bob but wanted to know what had happened to this person who had brought the message to Bill. Stunned by this coincidence, I just waved my arm toward the couch, and with a feeling of guilt, pointed to Ebby—out like a light. I then hurriedly motioned for the man to follow me and showed him in to see Bobbie.

Ebby was often an unhappy, even angry, man. When drunk, he expressed jealousy that Bill gave credit to Dr. Bob rather than himself as cofounder. Bill, on the other hand, was unfailingly loyal to Ebby, constantly concerned about his welfare. In the early sixties, after Ebby's return from Texas (where he had been sent by some New York members to AA members in Texas to help keep him sober), Bill planned to solicit the earliest old-timers who knew Ebby well, asking for whatever support they could give Ebby. This didn't materialize. But another plan did, involving LeRoy Chipman. When Mr. Chipman retired, he apparently had few financial resources. In gratitude for his contributions to AA, Bill had persuaded the trustees to provide an honorarium for him. This continued until it became evident that Ebby also desperately needed some regular financial assistance. So Bill visited the Rockefeller office and explained the situation. The Rockefeller people most readily agreed to assume Mr. Chipman's support. The AA honorarium then went to help Ebby in an upstate New York nursing home for the last couple years of his life, where he received tender, loving care from the managers of the home, Margaret and Mickey McP. until Ebby died in March 1966, ill but sober for two years. Bill and Lois visited him up there several times also.

A year before Ebby died, Bill shared some of his deep feelings about Ebby via a letter to an old friend, one of the earliest members in New York. Defending Ebby's worth to the fellowship, Bill said:

Of course, his service, one great one only, was the fact that he sponsored me. Had it not been for Ebby, whatever you may think of him personally, there probably wouldn't have been any AA at all. So in the minds of many, including myself, this does put him in a somewhat unique position. Besides, he has always been destitute, partly due to no business training and partly due to his drinking. At the present time, he has such a case of emphysema that he is an invalid, quite unable to take care of himself. . . . Because of these conditions and because he was my sponsor, I have tried to help him money-wise over the years. Perhaps this has done more harm than good, but under the circumstances, I couldn't do less. Had you been my sponsor, and were you destitute today, I would have done exactly the same for the same reason.

Bill always called Ebby his sponsor, inviting him to the New York Intergroup dinners and to the international conventions, where Bill introduced him, always giving him credit for helping Bill get sober by passing on the Oxford Group principles, which Bill expanded into what became the Twelve Steps of Alcoholics Anonymous.

As I said earlier, so many critically important and significant events occurred in that period immediately before and after I came to the office that I look back in awe. As he told me that first day, Bill was embroiled in a debate with the trustees regarding their place in the total AA picture and their relationship, their structural linkage—as well as his—and that of the office headquarters with the groups. He wrote many memos and created a "Code of Tradition," a "Code for Headquarters," and a "Code for the *Grapevine,*" setting forth his ideas of how the different elements of the structure could and should work together. He was pushing hard to promote self-government for the fellowship through a General Service Conference. There was a lot of controversy surrounding the idea.

As AA was growing, the office was growing too. By the end of 1949, we had six AA staff gals and fourteen other employees. Bill was traveling a lot and was in the office only one or two days a week when he was home. Hence, the office suffered from lack of overall management. To remedy this, the trustees that year appointed a General Service Committee to oversee the office on a day-to-day basis. Its chair, Hank G., was therefore the de facto volunteer manager of the office. It later became a salaried position, first on a part-time and eventually on a full-time basis. I remember Hank as a man of medium height, with a round face and rust-colored hair and mustache. He was an intense man, inclined to be gruff on occasion, but caring, and his contributions to the office were many and had a profound effect on headquarters operations. For example, his structure and program for the international conventions, which were held every five years following the initial one in Cleveland in 1950, were admired greatly by AAs and outside professionals alike and are still followed today.

I think the year 1950 was a particularly significant year in AA's history.

In one single year all the following events and more took place.

1. Early in the year, Bill made his last big trip out among the groups to promote the conference idea and Traditions. Lois usually had accompanied him on previous trips. This time, Bill realized clearly the extent of the families' involvement and the need for their own fellowship. Up to this point, our office had serviced these groups as they formed, putting them in touch with each

other and providing our pamphlet, "To Wives," taken from chapter 8 of the Big Book, *Alcoholics Anonymous*, and registering them in our files.

2. It was suggested to Lois that she coordinate the ninety or more "family" groups into a fellowship based on the Twelve Steps and Twelve Traditions. Anne B., as co-founder, assisted Lois in forming Al-Anon early in 1951.

3. Bill and Lois took a trip to Europe, where excitedly they saw the expansion of AA in other countries and the need for translations of AA literature and for service structures.

4. The First International Convention of AA was held in Cleveland, where the Traditions were accepted and Dr. Bob made his last talk and final appearance before he died.

5. Bill made his final and successful effort to persuade Bob to endorse the conference.

6. A memorial plaque was dedicated at St. Thomas Hospital, Akron, Ohio, by friends of Dr. Bob and Anne, to sisters and staff of the hospital. This marked Akron as the birthplace of Alcoholics Anonymous.

7. Dr. Bob passed away November 16, 1950.

8. The trustees at their fall meeting reluctantly agreed to test the conference idea. They endorsed the First Conference meeting to be held in April 1951.

9. The second *Saturday Evening Post* article by Jack Alexander appeared on March 29: "The Drunkard's Best Friend."

10. The headquarters office moved to larger quarters around the corner at 141 East Forty-Fourth Street.

Later that same year, in addition to my other duties, I began my work with Bill. I believe that came about because I was older than the other girls when I came to the office. I was a college graduate and ex-schoolteacher and perhaps had broader and different intellectual interests. The secretary who had been taking Bill's dictation resigned in 1950, and the demands on Bill's time had increased so enormously that he needed someone to be secretary, aide, and assistant combined. So Helen B. of the staff recommended me for the job. Although this ushered in the most exciting and fulfilling time of my life—thirty-two incredible years (to retirement) that I wouldn't take anything for—there was one disadvantage to the arrangement. On the one hand, I was still an employee of the headquarters office, continuing as receptionist for a few more years and handling many other responsibilities much later in the sixties. But on the other hand I was responsible primarily to Bill, keeping his correspondence up to date, helping with his writing projects, and assisting him at conferences and conventions.

During the early years of the General Service Conference sessions, I attended mainly to stay close to Bill—to answer questions, run errands, and so on. Prior to the very first meeting in April 1951, there was discussion at the office about stationing someone like a bouncer at the entrance to the meeting room (at the II Hotel Commodore) to watch for any unauthorized person who might try to attend the meetings. Some aggravation had been caused by a member from the Midwest who at first politely asked if he could attend. He was refused with regret because meetings were limited to only delegates, staff, and trustees. He called on us all again and still more times apparently, each time becoming more angry and strident, telling us we couldn't prevent him from attending any AA meeting, and so on. So things got a bit prickly, and it was decided to station someone at the door, someone who could distinguish delegates from nondelegates without too much debate. I was informed I had been chosen for this special and important duty. So the moment arrived—everyone filed into the meeting room except me. The door closed—and I waited in complete silence and expectation. Soon a large, tall man approached me and aggressively said he wanted to attend the meeting. I was a bit nervous, though enjoying the drama of it, too, and assured him meekly it wasn't possible. He tried again, and this time I stood up to my full height and firmly stated again I couldn't let him in. To my surprise, he backed down, and said something like, "Well, okay" and quickly walked away. I felt I had accepted a challenge and won! I often wonder who he was: the guy who threatened to challenge us, or someone from the area hearing about the conference.

When I started at the office, Bill was writing a series of essays for the *Grapevine,* the monthly AA journal, which was still in its infancy at that time. The essays were entitled "Twelve Points to Assure Our Future"—later to become AA's Twelve Traditions. Bill described these as "a set of general principles, simply stated, which offer tested solutions to all of AA's problems of living and working together and of relating our Society to the world outside." In 1952 Bill decided to combine the Traditions essays with a new series of essays on how each of the Steps applied to sober living, in the form of a hardcover book. I remember a moving letter that he dictated in July of that year to Father Ed Dowling in St. Louis in which he said,

> The problem of the Steps has been to broaden and deepen them, both for newcomers and oldtimers. . . . We have to deal with atheists, agnostics, believers, depressives, paranoids, clergymen, psychiatrists, and all and sundry. How to widen the opening so it seems right and reasonable to enter there and at the same time to avoid distractions, distortions, and the certain prejudices of all who may read, seems fairly much of an assignment.

Bill was himself one of the "depressives" he mentioned. He had that condition for much of the decade 1945–55 and was sometimes almost incapacitated by it. Sometimes when he was dictating to me slowly and with great difficulty, he would have to stop in midsentence, unable to go on. He would bury his face in his hands and weep in frustration. Yet that decade also saw an incredible outpouring of creativity and some of the greatest achievements of his life: the conference plan, acceptance of the Twelve Traditions, improvements in the service structure, assistance to the *Grapevine,* and many of his important writings. One of these achievements certainly was *Twelve Steps and Twelve Traditions* and following up plans for an important and ambitious writing project for AA.

Bill followed the same practice he had done with the Big Book. That is, he wrote a section at a time, and we sent it to friends and editors for their comments. Betty L., Tom P., and Jack Alexander (of the famous *Saturday Evening Post* articles about AA) were of particular help. As soon as *Twelve Steps and Twelve Traditions* was published in January 1953, it was an immediate success—to Bill's surprise. By October, twenty-five thousand copies had been shipped. It has remained AA's second best-selling book.

About this time, Bill got the idea of forming a "Writing and Research Team" consisting of the two of us plus Ed B., an alcoholic from a prominent family, who had had considerable success as a writer and editor before alcoholism ruined his career. The purpose of the team was to turn out several projects Bill had in mind:

1. A second edition of the Big Book, long anticipated. Bill was traveling to gather personal stories from old-timers but needed help in transcribing and editing them.

2. The full-length history of Alcoholics Anonymous. However, as Bill's depressions precluded this kind of commitment, this ended up as *AA Comes of Age* in 1957.

3. A book that would distill his and others' experience in applying the program to everyday living. Working title: *In All Our Affairs*. This idea eventually evolved into a book first entitled *The AA Way of Life* but now called *As Bill Sees It*. The *Grapevine's* recent book of Bill's *Grapevine* articles served nicely as a substitute for *In All Our Affairs*.

Our Writing and Research Team began working at 141 East Forty-Fourth Street, but the following year (1955) we moved to a space in a loft building at 305 East Forty-Fifth Street, adjacent to the shipping department, which had also been relocated there. The reason was partly to relieve the overcrowding at the General Service Office, but even more to get away from interruptions and distractions. We toiled diligently for a couple of years and produced the first two projects. Although Ed B.'s considerable talents were helpful, he often became frustrated at our indecisive writing schedule. Since Bill's projected writing program had to be curtailed, we let Ed go. So most of the time (until the 1960s, when G.S.O. moved over) I was all by myself at 305 East Forty-Fifth Street.

For the earlier projected history, Ed and I started digging into the old files and records of the office going all the way back to when it had started in 1940 down on 30 Vesey Street. Back in the forties, these files had been stored in a downtown warehouse but now were brought back up and stored in boxes on shelves reaching all the way to the ceiling in the shipping room outside our door. Bill encouraged me to continue the digging and sorting and to organize this material. He wrote once, "The whole story of AA is hidden in these boxes, waiting only to be searched out. . . . Thanks to our research activity, it is now certain that the basic facts of AA's growth and development can never be distorted." This "new undertaking of Nell's," as he called it, was the beginnings of the AA Archives. We made a start at it in 1957 and continued as time permitted until our actual formal beginning in 1972.

I said I was alone most of the time but that was not entirely true. As I started to weed through the old warehouse-stored files, I became aware that live inhabitants were in there—pesky little paper moths. They had lived and bred undisturbed for many years, happily hunkered down among the deteriorating papers. As I invaded their territory for the first time, they would suddenly leap out, stirring up little puffs of dust as they took flight. One time, Bill had brought a visitor over from Forty-Fifth Street. We started to chat, and at that very moment I felt something stirring inside my loose blouse. It felt like a large bee or a horsefly as it orbited back to front at a furious speed. I couldn't concentrate on what the visitor was saying, much less make sensible responses. Mercifully, maybe because of my strange twitching, he didn't stay too long. As soon as he disappeared, I frantically shed the blouse and out flew one of those tiny paper moths. (I've often wondered what kind of story that visitor shared with his group about Bill's weird secretary when he returned home.)

Some of my most vivid and touching memories of the early office were of our Christmas parties. Of course, AA was not against outsiders' drinking, and Bill and staff were always especially scrupulous about making sure that nonalcoholics were served drinks if they wanted them—which we all did. At one Christmas party the younger girls got a little tiddly and began flirting through the windows with some fellows having a party in their office (which happened to be that of Seagram Distillers) across the street in the Chrysler building. They were communicating with gestures and handwritten signs. Things went great until the men discovered the girls were from AA.

We would sing carols, exchange gifts (Bill was Santa), and play records for dancing. But the high point of every Christmas party was when Bill leaned back in his chair, hands in pockets, in the middle of the room and we quieted down, sitting on the floor at his feet to hear him tell how AA began—what he called his "bedtime story." This unique sense of unity, this small, close family, our special and cherished togetherness at this time, each Christmas in these early days, is something I'll always remember and cherish with gratitude. It was that first Christmas I knew I was bonded. I knew that Mexico would have to wait—perhaps for a long time.

In 1954 I began going up to Stepping Stones an average of every third weekend because Bill preferred to work there. I became friends with Lois, getting to know her better. After "work" on Saturday, the three of us took long walks together. In the evenings, we would have music—Bill playing the violin or cello and Lois or me accompanying him on the piano. Stepping Stones in time became my second home, and Bill and Lois were my family, closer really than my real parents, as I relied on them for advice and counsel in my occasional "affairs of the heart" and any problems as they occurred.

I got to know many, many other longtime, contributing figures in Alcoholics Anonymous history, as well.

4

"The People! Oh, the People!"

$\mathcal{S}$OBRIETY IN THE FORTIES didn't seem to be as stable and consistent as it is today. If a member slipped (hopefully temporarily), it was cause for disappointment or even despair. When a slip happened, Bill would say ruefully, "The people! Oh, the people! They won't stay fixed!"

Yet, to Bill people were not as often a cause of frustration as a cause of joy. He was unfailingly aware of the contributions made and role played by other people, nonalcoholics especially, to AA's cause and always gave full credit to others: to Lois, Ebby, Dr. Bob, Henrietta Seiberling, Dr. Harry Tiebout, Rockefeller friends, and so on. And never more so than at the Twentieth Anniversary International Convention in St. Louis in 1955. He wrote later, "At the Convention, it was widely appreciated for the first time that nobody had invented Alcoholics Anonymous, that many streams of influence and many people, some of them nonalcoholics, had helped by the grace of God, to achieve AA's purpose."

I attended the convention as Bill's secretary, as a "gofer" to run his errands; to help schedule lunch dates and visiting times, with people constantly pressing in on him; and to help out generally. Bill was simply everywhere during those three days and grew terribly tired. Me too! It was my first AA convention, and I was unprepared for the kick of being in the midst of a few thousand exuberant recovering alcoholics and friends of AA, and for the emotional wallop of the "coming of age" ceremony, marking the fellowship's acceptance of the charter of the General Service Conference. From today's perspective, it's hard for people to realize what a momentous decision was made that Sunday morning all those years ago, and the preparations for it. It was dramatic and extremely moving to us who knew what an effort of Bill's this was, over a lot of earlier opposition. He had pushed through the idea of a conference largely by campaigning for it personally. And a lot of members, particularly in the Midwest, still opposed the idea.

After Bill had presented his resolution, Bernard Smith, the chair, asked for a moment of silence for the crowd to invoke the guidance of God. Then Bern called for the vote, and a roar of approval went up.

Tears came to my eyes. I was sitting next to Dennis Manders, the nonalcoholic bookkeeper from the office. I could see that unshed tears filled his eyes too. (Dennis stayed at G.S.O. as long as I did, though our service years were different. He had become Controller and Chief Administrative Office of the huge operation when he retired in 1986.) We watched as Bill, to dramatize his stepping down, physically stepped down from the stage there in Kiel Auditorium. Dennis liked to kid about it later, saying "It took Bill twelve years to take that last step." It was true that Bill continued his custom of spending a day or two a week at G.S.O., and he was certainly involved with the trustee ratio dispute and many other issues until the late sixties. He also played a prominent part in the General Service Conferences, the 1969 World Service Meeting, and conventions during those years. And, of course, there were always voluminous piles of letters to answer. I worked with him throughout this whole time. But after 1955 he was at least freed from the day-to-day concerns of the office. (Incidentally, his decade-long depression gradually lifted in the months following the St. Louis Convention; within the next three or four years, he had regained a brighter outlook on life, helped in a great measure in the late fifties or early sixties by the vitamin therapy two of his friends, Dr. Abram Hoffer and Dr. Humphrey Osmond.)

So many figures who were important or crucial to AA's formative years were present there in St. Louis.

Ebby T., who first brought the message to Bill, was there as Bill's special guest. Bill arranged for Ebby to come up from Texas, where he had been living for almost a year. Caring for an alcoholic girl who eventually died left Ebby distraught, causing him to slip, then return to New York. But his six years of sobriety in Texas proved to be his longest dry period.

Another special guest was Bill's mother, "Dr. Emily." Even though she had divorced Bill's father when Bill was ten years old, Bill seemed eager to seek her approval all his life. So he wanted to have her present at this special convention to hear him speak and observe how people reacted to him. Bill said it was "the icing on the cake" for him.

Dr. Emily was a doctor of osteopathy living then in San Diego. Her second husband, Dr. Charles Strobel, a cancer specialist, had died in 1936. Beginning at age seventy-five, she also invested successfully in the stock market. Bill had given her shares in Portland Cement at the time he got into the stock market and she proved to be a smart investor, intuitively knowing when to buy and sell. When she lived with Bill and Lois for a while before she died, I was used to seeing her in bed early in the evening, knees drawn up, eyeglasses on top of her head, concentrated on her stock reports. I knew she was contemplating either buying or selling. The next morning, a decision was made—a phone call or maybe passing information to Bill. It turned out that her decision was right: If she decided to sell, the stock went down, and vice versa. She accumulated a fairly sizable estate, though she was careful in her living expenses. Bill nicknamed her "Hetty" after the famous Hetty Green, a gal who amassed a large fortune in the early part of the century and wielded an equally large amount of political power. Dr. Emily enjoyed the nickname.

I didn't see how Dr. Emily could have helped but be impressed with her son during that convention. But truthfully, she didn't show it overly much. When, however, she came to stay with Bill and Lois over a period during the last couple years of her life, she expressed deep devotion and appreciation for Bill's contributions to AA, and she enjoyed his AA friends. I saw a lot of her during those years, and we corresponded on other occasions, which I enjoyed. Her messages were short, pointed, and witty. She signed them with her usual "Heap Big Love." I became very fond of her.

As always, Lois contributed her ideas, enthusiasm, and energy to the St. Louis Convention—concentrating on her Al-Anon Family Groups' activities. But she was also at Bill's side whenever he needed her, and of course at the "Big Meeting." On the Sunday afternoon of the "coming of age," she was the first speaker to address the crowd in Kiel Auditorium after the epochal vote had been taken.

Austin MacCormick, the noted penologist, spoke at one of the panels in St. Louis. Dear Austin was everybody's favorite trustee, a smallish, kindly man who contributed so much to knowledge of medications of alcoholic prison inmates. He was absolutely devoted to Alcoholics Anonymous and an enormous help in promoting understanding among other leaders in the corrections field. He supported Bill loyally during the ratio debates in the following decade. In fact, he was just about the only supporter.

Dr. Sam Shoemaker was also at the convention. He was one of the contributing nonalcoholic friends of Bill and the fellowship. He was an Episcopal clergyman active in the Oxford Group whose teaching was so important in formulating the AA program. Bill used to talk about Dr. Sam's forthrightness and his utter honesty and sincerity. Bill said once that it was from Dr. Sam that he absorbed most of the principles that were embodied in the Twelve Steps. He once wrote, "Sam passed on the spiritual keys by which we were liberated." Dr. Sam was charismatic—a tall, good-looking man, a little portly, with a strong voice. An articulate speaker, he made a marvelous talk in St. Louis that, along with several others, is carried in *AA Comes of Age*. Dr. Shoemaker having long since passed away, I went over to Austin, Texas, and spent some time in the Episcopal Church archives, with permission of Dr. Sam's wife, Helen Shoemaker, searching for any missing letters between Dr. Sam and Bill. I brought back a batch of material, including some that shed new light on the controversy between Frank Buchman, a leader of the Oxford Group, and Dr. Shoemaker. Their association ended in 1941.

Another important church leader present was Father Ed Dowling. He was from St. Louis. He had learned of AA in 1940 while visiting Chicago members. Back in St. Louis, he had helped start the first AA group. Bill called Father Ed his "spiritual sponsor" and "a friend, advisor, great example, and the source of more inspiration than I can say." When he introduced the Catholic priest to speak, Bill said, "Father Ed is made of the stuff of saints." I admired Father Ed myself because he was direct and full of humor, and he exuded a deep spirituality, humility, and consideration and thoughtfulness of other people. He was of medium height with a wide "map of Ireland" face and a shock of white hair. Because of a limp, he walked with a cane. (When Father Ed died, he gave his cane and his personal crucifix to Bill. They were among Bill's favorite and most cherished possessions and are still to be seen in his studio at Stepping Stones.)

Leonard Harrison, who was a trustee of the Alcoholic Foundation (later changed to the General Service Board) and its chair in the forties, participated in the convention on opening day. He was a sociologist by profession, a fine-looking gentleman with thinning white hair, always dignified and calm. Bill called him "one of AA's oldest and most valued friends, who saw it through its frightfully wobbly time of adolescence, when nobody could say whether our society would hang together or blow up." He was describing the situation as it was when I came to work at the office.

Dr. Leonard Strong couldn't make it to St. Louis, which disappointed Bill. Dr. Strong was Bill's brother-in-law, married to Bill's sister, Dorothy. When almost everyone else had deserted Bill and Lois, he had seen them through the worst of Bill's drinking and made possible the linkage for Bill with Charles Towns Hospital and Dr. William Silkworth. Later, he was the absolutely essential link between Bill and the people around John D. Rockefeller, Jr., through his old friend the Reverend Willard Richardson, who handled Mr. Rockefeller's private charities. This connection led directly to the formation in 1938 of the Alcoholic Foundation and its board of trustees. It is no exaggeration to say that without Dr. Strong's loving concern for Bill, there might not have been a fellowship called Alcoholics Anonymous!

I have known Leonard and Dorothy Strong for forty years or more. In my early days at the office, I occasionally took some special dictation from him, when he was secretary of the Alcoholic Foundation, until his retirement from the board in 1955.

He always spoke in a low, soft voice, kind of a mumble; thank heavens my ears were in better shape then than they are now. Dr. Strong was formal on occasion, dignified—perhaps you could say a bit stuffy—but he had a grand sense of humor and loved to share jokes. He was also a bit feisty and wasn't in total agreement with Bill's idea of a General Service Conference.

I remember many visits with Bill and Lois to the Strongs when they lived near White Plains, New York, years ago. Dot was a great cook. Her New England–style dinners were especially enjoyable and tasty. Leonard, before dinner, would appear wearing his smart smoking jacket, a curved pipe in his mouth, very British, gentlemanly, blowing gentle puffs of smoke, eyes twinkling as he and we all engaged in sharing favorite stories and conversation about AA or personal happenings.

I kept in touch with these dear people until recently, especially Dorothy, who was a warm, lovely, caring person. For many years, we talked on the telephone about once a month, shared news of Bill and Lois and Stepping Stones events. Of course she was a regular contact with the Wilsons also. They loved the Strongs so dearly and always expressed tremendous gratitude to Leonard for his faith in Bill and for his firm support of Bill's efforts to start AA by making possible, as I said earlier, the contact with the Rockefeller people at the end of 1937.

Well up into their eighties, Leonard and Dot lived at the Brandon Inn in Brandon, Vermont, then later both had to enter at different times a nursing home in nearby Rutland. Leonard was first to go, having had a stroke that impaired his speech seriously. Dorothy, living by herself, suffered a fall down a flight of steps and was placed in the same nursing home with Leonard. But the fall affected Dorothy's memory, so their later days were difficult, for them as well as their friends. I still feel grief, calling Dot and facing her lack of recognition. She is surrounded though, with many loving friends and family. Leonard died April 24, 1989. (So many longtime friends have "passed from our sight and hearing," as Bill often put it during the past years.) Dot was aware of his passing and seemed to recover somewhat from loss of memory.

I have always felt that people who worked for Mr. John D. Rockefeller, Jr., in his private charities division never received sufficient credit for the crucial part they played in AA's beginning. As I mentioned before, the Reverend Willard Richardson was one who also became a close personal friend of Bill and Lois—we called him "Uncle Dick." Bill called him "one of the finest servants of God and man I shall ever know." He was the key person who persuaded Mr. Rockefeller, Jr., to contribute to the support of the "small bunch of alcoholics," later hosting the famous Rockefeller dinner for AA in 1940. Mr. Rockefeller couldn't attend at the last minute but sent his son Nelson to read his remarks—which praised AA warmly but also said he believed that money would spoil it, which must have brought a momentary sense of disappointment to the alcoholic listeners, to say the least. However, Mr. Rockefeller did provide a thousand dollars. There were also donations from the other dinner guests to help the Alcoholic Foundation strengthen its shaky base. He also allowed the foundation to solicit the dinner guest list annually until 1945, when the groups started to contribute regularly. As Bill said in April 1945:

> It was a great day when lately the Trustees were able to express our profound thanks to Mr. Rockefeller and other friends and tell them that no more contributions were needed. It meant that the Foundation was no longer, to any degree a charitable enterprise. From that moment AA, nationally speaking, stood on its own feet, backed by the earning power of its own publications and the earning power of its 15,000 members.

Certainly this event marked a turning point in AA's growth and history.

The Reverend Richardson brought Frank Amos, a newspaper executive who had been sent by Mr. Rockefeller in 1937 to Akron to meet Dr. Bob and see what was going on there. His glowing report was the clincher in getting Mr. Rockefeller's support. Frank went on to be an enthusiastic and active trustee until his death in July 1965. I felt close to Frank and his wife, Mary, because they were later interested in psychic phenomena—as I am.

LeRoy "Chippie" Chipman was another one. He had been on Mr. Rockefeller's staff as treasurer of private charities and was in on the very first meeting that Leonard Strong helped to set up. As treasurer of the Alcoholic Foundation almost from its beginning, Chippie worked out the finances by paying off the early shareholders of the Big Book so that the foundation could take over Works Publishing. Later on he was also in general charge of the money side of the office. He wrote the checks, made the bank deposits, that sort of thing. Chippie was a shy little man, fussy and fastidious. He was perhaps a bit hard on the bookkeepers who reported to him, but a lovely man. He had twinkly eyes and a good sense of humor, like Leonard Strong. I remember how he loved to talk about the trip of his life, to New Zealand. After Chippie retired and was in poor health, Bill got the foundation to arrange an honorarium, to express their gratitude for Chippie's long and valuable service on behalf of the fellowship as well as work at the foundation office. Chippie was terribly disappointed that he was too ill to attend the St. Louis Convention.

Mr. Rockefeller remained in contact with Bill and AA until his death in 1960. I want to reproduce just a few words to show his admiration for Bill, from a Christmas message, December 21, 1949.

How gratifying it must be to you to know how many people your organization has helped and is continuing to help! Your leadership throughout has been an inspiration.

Bill was proud that Dr. Harry Tiebout, the first psychiatrist to recognize the work of AA and to use AA's principles in his own practice, had come all the way from Greenwich, Connecticut, to share with us at the convention. In 1939, Dr. Tiebout had seen spectacular AA recoveries in two of his patients, Marty M. and her friend Grennie C. (Grennie became a cherished friend of mine and we kept in close touch for many years until his death.) Dr. Tiebout became an enthusiastic supporter of AA and helped persuade two medical societies to invite Bill to read papers on it at their meetings. He also wrote a number of classic professional papers on AA himself and also for the *Grapevine*, which are still circulated and often quoted. (Two years after the convention, he was elected a trustee and served until his death in 1966.) Harry was a heavyset, genial man, easy to know, articulate, full of humor but firm in his convictions—sometimes in agreement with Bill's ideas, sometimes not. Bill praised his "penetrating insights," and I would concur. A really great man!

Bernard Smith was chair of the convention. He was also Chair of the Board Trustees at that time. A New York lawyer, he had helped in 1943 to change the board from a simple trust setup to a membership corporation. He had supported and also helped Bill put together the proposed General Service Conference structure. Bill called him "the architect of the Conference." When Bill was trying to push through the idea of the conference, Bern Smith was the only trustee supporting him. It was he who finally brought a majority of the other trustees around to accept the conference on a trial basis. Stocky in build, quick in wit and mind, perceptive, he relished a few drinks. He sometimes referred to himself as a "so-called non-alcoholic." He was devoted to Bill and to AA.

Another of the true giants in AA history who was at St. Louis—and at every AA International Convention ever held—was Dr. John L. Norris, known throughout AA as "Dr. Jack." Dr. Jack was a handsome, white-haired, soft-spoken New England Yankee—the prototype board chair right out of central casting. As Associate Medical Director of Eastman Kodak in Rochester, New York, he was a pioneer not only in industrial medicine but also in alcoholism. He saw at first hand some remarkable AA recoveries, became a believer, and got to meet Bill in 1942 or 1943. Bill invited Dr. Jack to join the board in 1950. He was to remain a trustee until his death at age eighty-five on January 13, 1989—an active member for twenty-seven years and emeritus for ten. And he was Chair of the Board for seventeen years, through AA's great growth and greatest problems. During the entire thirty-seven years, I don't believe he ever missed a board meeting unless he was ill or abroad, nor a General Service Conference. I have known and admired Dr. Jack nearly my entire AA life and could not have more respect and affection for him—even though as chair he was frequently at odds with Bill on various issues. But he had the courage of his convictions.

Nell with the AA Big Book.

5

Bill W. at Work: His Contributions

*P*EOPLE SOMETIMES EXPRESS surprise that during most of those years I worked with Bill W., my desk was located in his extra-large office. This was true both at the AA headquarters and at Stepping Stones, and sometimes in the studio that he and a neighbor built about fifty yards from the main house. He called this workplace "Wit's End." (The choice of the name can really be attributed to Lois.) Thus I was not only close by to help with whatever he was doing, but I was also there during his conversations over the phone or with visitors and during meetings. Recently someone theorized that since Bill was aware of the importance of the AA movement he had founded, and because of my own sense of AA as a sociohistorical movement, perhaps he wanted me to be an "eyewitness to history."

Interesting, but I don't think so. Remember, Bill had grown up in conservative and traditional New England in the early part of the century. In those days, it was not unusual for a small-town banker, lawyer, and business executive to have his clerk or secretary work in a corner of his office. It was a sort of status symbol as well as more convenient before the days of intercoms, Dictaphones, and word processors. In the overcrowded

AA offices in the middle years, it was also a matter of using every square foot of space as efficiently as possible. And even when the G.S.O. space expanded greatly, giving us a big office in later years, Bill and I continued with the status quo.

Out of those many years of close proximity and firsthand observation of Bill in the large offices at G.S.O. locations and Stepping Stones have come some thoughts about his perceptive and extraordinary contributions to Alcoholics Anonymous—and to other areas of human problems that benefited from following the philosophy and experience of AA.

First was his amazing foresightedness. Instead of being totally distracted by the myriad details, squabbles, and tempests in a teapot that characterized early AA, Bill always thought in terms of the "big picture." His eyes were at least three quarters of the time focused on the future, not on the daily "niggles and naggles," as he called them. He had the ability to extrapolate from current or past experiences and foresee the consequences of events. Then he would push for ideas that would help the fellowship develop and grow and reach alcoholics worldwide. His and Lois's trip abroad in 1950 spurred this insight into this larger reality.

For example, many of the early groups made every mistake in the books. Some of them put restrictions on who could join. Others imposed membership rules after people came in. Still others got involved in hospitals or lobbied for changes in laws that applied to alcoholics—all of which led to confusion externally and strife internally. And I've already mentioned the problems caused by Bill's "endorsements" of NCEA and various public figures' disregard of anonymity, going public with their AA membership.

Bill, instead of becoming mired down in these problems of the early 1940s, took the advice of Earl T., founder of AA in Chicago, to codify this decade of experience. Bill was able to synthesize it into a set of guidelines for the survival, unity, and effectiveness of the fellowship. "On the anvils of experience," he said, "the structure of our society was hammered out." Characteristically, he first called these guidelines "Twelve Points to Assure Our Future;" later he began to call them "Traditions." Had he tried to call them rules or regulations, they might never have been accepted. That was another trait of Bill's—using the right descriptive word or phrase.

Then he took the Traditions out to the fellowship in the later part of the forties, to try to "sell" them to the groups. They didn't want to listen. I recall one instance that Bill loved to tell on himself. When planning a trip, he had written ahead to let the groups know he was coming to their town. They wrote back something like, "We would love to have you come and speak. Tell us about that hot flash spiritual experience of yours, but please don't talk any more about those d—— Traditions." But the fellowship did formally adopt them in the Short Form (reduced by Bill in 1949) at the Cleveland Convention in 1950.

Another significant contribution by Bill was how he learned to communicate his own recovery—or "to share his experience, strength, and hope," as AA puts it—with other alcoholics. You'll recall that after Bill left Towns Hospital, he tried to preach (as Dr. Silkworth described it) to every alcoholic he could find, totally without success. But when he shared his own experience with the drunken Dr. Bob out at Akron, he was able to help both Dr. Bob and himself. Afterward, his extraordinary ability to communicate the wretchedness and despair of his own drunkenness and to inspire other alcoholics with his soaring spiritual awakening spurred their recovery in turn and led them to share their own experience, strength, and hope with the next prospect—thus spreading Alcoholics Anonymous to the ends of the earth.

Bill loved to talk—no doubt about that! His hold on audiences was almost hypnotic. Sometime in the sixties, I was sitting with Herb M., the general manager of G.S.O., at one of the annual "Bill's Birthday Dinners" that the New York Intergroup sponsored and still does. Herb could occasionally be critical of some of Bill's ideas; they sparred verbally on occasion. So this night, I was surprised to catch Herb drying his eyes and blowing his nose (as were hundreds of other AAs in the huge audience) as Bill finished speaking. Herb shook his head in admiration at how articulate Bill could be. He reached everybody he talked to.

In Bill's talks he brought out the need for an alcoholic to reach bottom before an inner spiritual change could be achieved. Stressing this idea of "deflation at depth" as a prerequisite to recovery was another of Bill W.'s great contributions. From the Oxford Groups he got the concept of surrendering one's will to a Higher Power before one could obtain guidance. And William James's *The Varieties of Religious Experience* suggests how a deflation of ego almost always precedes a spiritual awakening. Bill's contribution was the realization that this "reaching a bottom," so to speak, was the key to recovery for the alcoholic. Later, Dr. Tiebout in his professional papers attributed much of AA's success to this idea. In the Big Book, Bill describes alcoholic behavior as "self-will run riot" and states, "self-centeredness is the root of our problem." Hence Step One of the Twelve Steps confronts the need for ego deflation at depth head-on: "We admitted we were powerless over alcohol—that our lives had become unmanageable." In explaining this Step further in the Twelve Steps and Twelve Traditions book, Bill wrote, "Only through utter defeat are we able to take our first steps toward liberation and strength. Our admissions of personal powerlessness finally turn out to be firm bedrock upon which happy and purposeful lives may be built."

Of course there were his many philosophical, organizational, and tangible contributions.

There were his books—written, granted, with the input and

help of others, but his books nonetheless: *Alcoholics Anonymous* and *Twelve Steps and Twelve Traditions,* of course, the real cornerstone of the AA program. *Alcoholics Anonymous Comes of Age—*which, as I mentioned, Ed B. and I helped put together. (Tom P. was overall editor.) It's a tour de force. I think of it as a vast canvas on which Bill paints a panorama of everything that had happened in AA from its birth until the St. Louis Convention and a portrait of AA's place in the world in 1955. *Twelve Concepts for World Service* (I remember well the four years of work on this one) on authority, responsibility, and leadership in AA and the interrelationship of the groups, the trustees, the conference, and the G.S.O. and *Grapevine.* His last book, *As Bill Sees It,* is a collection of quotations and excerpts from the books just mentioned plus his *Grapevine* articles and letters, the selection and production of which he guided himself. By the late sixties, Bill's emphysema was curtailing his activities, and Janet G. was a great help in researching my archival files and putting the book together for Bill.

In October 1988 the *Grapevine* published a large, four-hundred-page volume of all Bill W.'s writings in their pages since 1944, entitled *The Language of the Heart.* I admit to prejudice because they initially asked me to share some thoughts on it, but it's a perfectly marvelous work that reveals so much about Bill's own growth spiritually and his insight over the years. Actually, I consider it a fine substitute for the proposed last book Bill wanted so desperately to do—a summing up of his AA experience. Because of his emphysema problem, we couldn't accomplish it. It contains splendid examples of his leadership as well as AA's experience and history. I'm sure it will become one of AA's basic resources. Bill's words speak to us just as directly today as they did when he wrote them twenty, thirty, forty years ago.

There were his structural aims, such as corporate poverty,

lack of any personal authority at all ("our leaders are but trusted servants"), and the minimum organization possible to carry the message. People said that such ridiculous ideas would never work, but they do. After Bill's death, Lois and I talked about where he got these ideas. She believed the teachings of St. Francis of Assisi specifically influenced his thinking along these lines. Bill probably became interested in St. Francis through Father Ed Dowling or "Sister" Frances, the original owners of Ken Farm, Connecticut, for problem people, and came to admire the saint for his organization yet spirituality. Bill was proud to tell people that A A was an anarchy; a benevolent anarchy, he would say, but an anarchy nevertheless.

There was his recognition of the danger of single-person leadership. In this, Bill was influenced by reading about Mary Baker Eddy, the Christian Science leader. An early teacher and mentor accused her of failure to give him proper credit for certain critical ideas that she adopted as an integral part of her teaching. The resulting controversy was harmful. From Bill's folders in the archives I remember especially a 1943 letter from Bill to a friend alluding to this incident, in which he said:

> No one in A A should ever be subjected to such temptations.
> . . . A A should always give full credit to its several well-springs
> of inspiration and should always consider these people
> among the founders of our well-loved society.

Bill himself certainly set an example in giving credit to others, belying doubts about his lack of humility.

From this recognition of the danger of single leadership followed his insistence on group autonomy. He explained that meant simply that every A A group is free to manage its affairs exactly as it pleases unless it threatens A A as a whole. I have heard him say again and again, "Every group has a right to be wrong."

Although AA seems to have grown much more rigid since Bill's death, he was unbelievably tolerant and permissive himself. One day a delegation of members came all the way from a Midwestern city to fill Bill's ear with the troubles they were having with some old tyrants who were running a clubhouse for AAs just the way they pleased, and they wanted Bill to do something about it. This bunch, they said, was using the group's money for other purposes, excluding members they didn't like, and I don't know what all. It all sounded pretty bad to me as I eavesdropped from my desk. But Bill just put his long legs up on the desk, leaned back in his chair and thought a while. Finally he asked, "Are these guys sober?" The delegation admitted, yes they were. Bill just looked at them and said, "Well . . ." And that was the end of the interview.

The whole evolution of a linkage, or corporate structure for providing AA services, can be credited to Bill's vision, persuasion, and persistence. Confusion reigned during the late forties and fifties with every element of service performing separate operations. It was like a human body with the head and the limbs disconnected from the torso. The trustees were doing their own thing; they conceived of their responsibility as primarily custodial; they were not an "action" body. They were at first wary of the conference idea and later of the conference itself. The conference delegates were new to the job, and although they understood they were responsible for the whole operation, they were somewhat in awe of the trustees, many of them having had no direct connection to the office. As I said before, the AA staff members at the office functioned pretty much on their own and in the forties weren't entirely sure of their status. The *Grapevine* was off by itself in that little structure of its own and apparently responsible to nobody.

Bill with his vision foresaw that this lack of linkage of services and lack of direct cooperation could lead to internal conflict and contained the seeds of possible destruction of Alcoholics

Anonymous. Having pushed through the idea of a General Service Conference, with the "final responsibility and ultimate authority" in the hands of the groups, Bill then tried to pull together all these disparate elements into what he termed the "Third Legacy of Service" (the first two Legacies being Recovery and Unity, through the Twelve Steps and the Twelve Traditions, respectively). He put together a Third Legacy Manual, later enlarged and edited, renamed *The AA Service Manual*. It explains how the whole structure works. It's a treasure in my opinion, and I guess the fellowship agrees because it is followed faithfully and is reissued nearly every year with changes and revisions directed by the conference. The manual, however, was essentially a nuts-and-bolts guide, and Bill felt something more was needed.

Therefore, in 1959 he began to write a supplement to the manual "to record the why of our service structure in such a fashion that the highly valuable experience of the past, and the lessons we have drawn from that experience, can never be forgotten or lost." How typically "Bill" that statement is. To this day, not too many know much about the writing of *The Twelve Concepts for World Service,* as Bill called the document. Probably more than any other of his books, this represents completely his personal thinking—a final contribution of quality leadership. He wrote out the entire manuscript in longhand, painfully working it over, deleting, inserting, changing as he went. He then handed me the pages of script to type up. As the conference finally approved and published it in 1962, it is the only piece of AA literature that bears his or any other individual's byline. The concepts are clearly labeled "by Bill W."

By this time he was free of day-to-day concerns pertaining to the office, so he was able to turn his attention to this effort, to which he gave a high priority. He had emerged from his depression and was able to concentrate clearly and with great insights. The concepts codify some of the spiritual principles already generally observed in AA, such as the "Right of Decision," the "Right of Participation," the "Right of Appeal" and so on. The concepts define the "responsibility and authority" of the groups and the role of the conference and the trustees. The concepts caution against "double-headed management," state the necessity of good personal leadership, and describe the working relationships of the service entities. Finally, Concept XII emphasizes and elaborates on the "General Warranties of the Conference." (As these are Article 12 of the Conference Charter, they were undoubtedly the joint product of Bern Smith and Bill.) I'd like to quote them here, as they are one of the most remarkable documents I've ever read:

> In all its proceedings, the General Service Conference shall observe the spirit of the AA Tradition, taking great care that the Conference never becomes the seat of perilous wealth or power; that sufficient operating funds, plus an ample reserve, be its prudent financial principle; that none of the Conference members shall ever be placed in a position of unqualified authority over any of the others; that all important decisions be reached by discussion, vote, and whenever possible, by substantial unanimity; that no Conference action ever be personally punitive or an incitement to public controversy; that, though the Conference may act for the service of Alcoholics Anonymous, it shall never perform any acts of government; and that, like the Society of Alcoholics Anonymous which it serves, the Conference itself will always remain democratic in thought and action.

When they were introduced, the Twelve Concepts were greeted with indifference—followed by years of virtual neglect. After all, they applied mainly to those involved in service, and besides they were extremely tough reading. I recall that the AA staff at the office were given a study course in the concepts prior to the conference. However, there has been a renaissance of interest in the Concepts in the last decade. On being invited to AA conventions or regional service get-togethers, I have been enormously pleased to see that workshops on the Concepts created a lot of interest. For they—and the structure they describe—are one of Bill's greatest contributions.

In light of the vast self-help movements that have developed, Bill's openness to sharing AA principles, AA's Twelve Steps, and AA's experience with other Twelve Step fellowships must be regarded as one of his most far-reaching contributions. It started with his recognition of the need for families of alcoholics to have their own separate fellowship, and he encouraged Lois to form the Al-Anon family groups. Soon the AA experience had spread to help solve almost any human problem you can name: emotional illness, schizophrenia, gambling, overeating, narcotics—specifically cocaine—addiction, sexual obsession, compulsive debting, and so on. Self-help groups exist for widows and widowers, parents who have lost a child, parents of children with Down's Syndrome, survivors of mastectomies (I participate in one of these myself) and other cancers, and victims of most other chronic illnesses. The total membership in such self-help groups is estimated in tens of millions. And it all started with Alcoholics Anonymous and Bill's willingness to share its programs with anyone who would be helped by it. After all, he said everything in AA is borrowed from somewhere else; so why shouldn't we be willing to share it with others? That policy is still followed today. Note, however, that Bill opposed the creation of multiproblem groups within AA itself (such as drug and alcohol groups or "addictions anonymous" groups).

And that policy is still followed today as well.

For my part, however, Bill W.'s greatest contribution of all was his willingness—even eagerness—to step down as leader. From the first time I met him until his death, he devoted a large part of his energy and time to trying to divest himself of power and authority, instead of trying to hang onto them. This idea was an integral part of the Twelve Traditions. Tradition Two states, "For our group purpose there is but one ultimate authority—a loving God as He may express Himself in our group conscience. Our leaders are but trusted servants; they do not govern." The General Service Conference grew out of this same idea—and Bill had to struggle long and hard to educate the groups to accept the power and authority. This is even more remarkable since it seemed contrary to Bill's own nature. He certainly had a healthy ego, which he constantly suppressed, and he frequently called himself a power-driver. And in this regard, I think he stands absolutely unique among the charismatic leaders of great movements. Most of them hang on until they either die or are forcefully unseated. But not Bill. Dear Dr. Jack summed it up in his eulogy: "He was willing to let go of us before we were willing to let go of him."

Nell Wing with Lois Wilson (at right), 1983.

6

Bill and Lois at Leisure

On my weekends at Stepping Stones, more often than not we would work upstairs: Lois working on Al-Anon at her desk, Bill dictating to me. Or, if he was through dictating, he might be napping on the couch while I was doing typing or filing. Other times Bill and I would be at the same routine in the studio up the hill, while Lois would spend hours in her beloved garden.

When our work was through, we usually took a walk or went for a drive. Bill would say to Lois, "Daddles, I'll drive." To which Lois would reply, "No, Bill. I'll drive." They would go back and forth like that a few times because driving was a relaxation for both of them. But Lois usually prevailed; she was perhaps the better driver of the two. Meanwhile, I would make myself comfortable in the backseat. On these long walks and longer car rides, especially in spring and fall, I got to know that beautiful, wooded Westchester countryside, all the lanes and roads. Some were still in their natural, unimproved state. I'm grateful for those times.

When we returned, Lois usually busied herself in the kitchen preparing the evening meal (she was a good steak-and-potatoes kind of cook), though in later years, Harriet was in the kitchen. At that point, Bill would turn to me and say, "Well, Nell, how about some of the old chestnuts?" I would sit down at the piano, he would pick up his violin or cello, and we would get right into favorites like "Home Sweet Home," "Roamin' in the Gloamin'," or "It's a Long Way to Tipperary" from his war years. "The Wearing of the Green" was a favorite and he wedged in "Seeing Nellie Home" if I was there.

Music was an important part of leisure time at Stepping Stones. Both Bill and Lois enjoyed classical music and kept the radio tuned most of the time to WQXR, the classical music station in New York. Lois had taken piano lessons as a girl in Brooklyn and played well—much better than I, although I too had had piano lessons back in Kendall, for which I was now grateful. Bill's grandfather had challenged him to learn the violin when he was just a lad. So he did, first rebuilding an old fiddle he had found in the attic. It had belonged to his Uncle Clarence. He taught himself to play by pasting a diagram on the neck of the fiddle and then sawing away until the right notes emerged. He spent hours listening to records, including violin solos, on the Victrola, after which he would return to his own practice.

He taught himself well enough to play first violin in the high school orchestra, which performed for school dances. He belittled this accomplishment by saying, "I was a very bad first violin in a very poor orchestra." Nevertheless, music continued to provide him a satisfying outlet for the rest of his life. I heard that he once took his violin on a visit to Dr. Bob and Anne in Akron, playing perhaps longer than they had anticipated. For years at the annual Al-Anon picnics at Stepping Stones, he would stroll among the guests on the lawn, playing his violin like a roving gypsy. Actually, he was better on the cello. I always believed if he had really pursued this instrument he could have had a successful career. He loved to listen to performances by Pablo Casals on records or on the radio, as did Lois. (In fact, right to the end Lois listened to the classical radio stations day and night.)

The piano, violin, and cello can still be seen in the corner of the living room at Stepping Stones.

Bill owned two violins. The second one was a gift from a pioneer member named Gib K. in Milwaukee. Bill and Lois visited there the year after I came to the office. Gib was in the hospital, terminally ill with cancer when Bill visited him. Gib pressed Bill to accept the violin as a last gift, so Bill treasured it. Besides playing these instruments, he was constantly tinkering with them, taking them apart and putting them together again. This was his engineering side taking over from his musical side. That is, besides trying to play the violin as well as possible, he felt impelled to make the instrument itself produce the optimum sound.

At Stepping Stones, I had the downstairs bedroom, a step up and just beyond the living room. I remember being kept awake until all hours more than one night while Bill tinkered with his violin in the living room, sawing away on the strings as he made adjustments. One of the violins he tinkered to death. Finally, it wouldn't stand any more "improvement" and refused to sound its A note.

Bill and Lois were both great walkers. When they first moved to Bedford Hills in 1941, they were practically the only people in the area, so they created their own walking trails up hill and down dale. As time passed, more and more people settled there, gradually moving almost to their doorstep—or would have if Bill and Lois had not been foresighted enough to purchase some of the surrounding acreage over succeeding years. But even when the area became more populated, they managed to keep portions of their original trails, which now sometimes wound through well-tended lawns or side yards, under the kitchen windows of the new neighbors. As Bill was a familiar sight, people would hail him from their porches or lawns or kitchen windows, and he would stop to chat with them. I remember the first time I strolled with them on a neighbor's now-private property, voicing the opinion that we might be trespassing. Not to worry! The neighbor called out waving, not minding the intrusion at all. They all liked Bill and Lois.

In Bill's best years when he was feeling vigorous, he could manage to do five miles a day. This was the period when I first began working at Stepping Stones. I remember one Saturday around 1954. Lois wasn't walking with us for some reason, perhaps she was recovering from her heart attack then. I was hiking along with Bill, and when we had covered about three miles, Bill was apparently surprised I could keep up. He turned to me and said, "Gosh, Nell, for a girl of your age you're a pretty good walker." Since I was thirty-seven at the time, I was kind of surprised he thought me so old, considering his own age—until I realized he was kidding!

His walking was a lifeline for him in those years of his sometimes crippling depressions. On days when he could scarcely get up out of bed, he would force himself to walk, taking deep breaths, putting one foot in front of the other, breathing and walking. Today I read many articles by doctors and psychologists recommending walking and other forms of exercise as the best possible therapy for maintaining good physical and mental health, and of special value to depressives. Bill was instinctively ahead of his time, as always.

Lois was just as dedicated a walker herself. She and I kept up the walks for many years after Bill died and until her health became too fragile for the long exercises. Usually we took shorter hikes by then, but we managed fairly long ones in the spring and fall. Lois was especially fond of the spring season, when we would inventory the winter's damage to the property: the broken branches and wild undergrowth that needed to be cleared at the outer edges of the property. (This was always Lois's concern rather than Bill's. Occupied totally with AA, he just wasn't as interested in the property and didn't give a lot of attention to its needs.) She loved viewing up close the first emergence of the tiniest baby leaves of the trees and bushes—the pink and white buds of the magnolias and dogwoods. This was always a tender and even spiritual adventure for me. On those chilly days in late March we would walk all around the property, always with the same sense of awe at the annual, mysterious unfolding of mother nature's fresh young season.

In the fall, when the air was soft and mellow, Lois and I would drink in the beauty of the autumn colors and would pick huge white and purple hydrangeas for the house—and some for me to take back to my New York apartment. I've learned so much from Lois—she was especially in harmony with her environment. She knew the names of all the trees, plants, and birds—birdfeeders all around the place. It was a constant battle of wits with the squirrels—and usually the squirrels won! Lois was a great teacher.

One episode in the fall of 1969 or spring of 1970 moves me deeply even as I write about it today. Bill's health had deteriorated by this time, and this was one of his few good days. The three of us started on a walk, deciding to try out a new, hilly road. At one point, Lois and I stopped to examine an unfamiliar species of flower. As Lois was telling me about it, I turned to see Bill walking on ahead of us, trudging along the upgrade, hands clasped behind his back, leaning forward as he always did. As his figure became smaller in the distance, I experienced a sudden but not unexpected premonition that this was to be the last walk the three of us would take together—which it was. I saw in that vision that Bill was literally and symbolically much ahead of us, while Lois and I were still attached to the things of this world, so to speak—to the roadside flowers and plants and nature. A moment later, Bill moved out of our sight.

7

What Bill Was Like: His Mind and Heart

*T*O UNDERSTAND THE AA MEM-
bers' view of Bill W. and Dr.
Bob, nonalcoholics should—and most do—understand that
AAs feel they would not be sober nor, indeed would they be
alive, if it were not for the cofounders. Because the fellowship
of AA grows almost entirely by a one-on-one process in which a
sober member helps the newcomer who is still suffering, it is literally possible for nearly every one of the millions of AA members around the world to trace his or her recovery directly back
through the chain of sponsors to the founders. Small wonder
then, that AAs tend to idolize Bill W. and while he was alive,
sought to meet him and thank him personally for their lives. As
archivist, I have met thousands of members who visited the
archives just to be reminded of where it all started. More often
than not, they find the experience emotional.

The same attitude characterizes the view of Al-Anon members toward their cofounder, Lois W.

As I am a member of neither Alcoholics Anonymous nor Al-
Anon, my perspective is somewhat different. My relationship
with Bill and Lois was more that of a quasi family member. They
had no children (Lois had suffered three ectopic pregnancies

71

with accompanying surgery, and they were unable to adopt because of Bill's alcoholism in those days), and they filled mother and father roles for me. I could talk to them about things I couldn't with my real parents. (My father had died in 1945; and my mother, who admired Bill and Lois and AA exceedingly, died in January 1971, a week before Bill, actually. I felt as if I had lost both parents.) Bill was my advisor and mentor, in some ways a father figure, but in other ways more of a big brother. Lois was an especially caring, dear friend, and mother figure too—the person whose friendship I treasured so deeply.

Once, I returned to New York from a vacation trip, stunned by the sudden death of my longtime friend, whom I was about to marry. Bill and Lois drove down from Bedford Hills to pick me up and take me back to Stepping Stones, where for many days they comforted me as best they could. Another time I was caught by an appendicitis attack and rushed to the hospital. Bill dashed down to be sure I was okay and after the operation and recovery period, took me back to Stepping Stones for recuperation. These are only a couple of examples of their loving concern for me. And the same caring attention was given to so many other relatives, close friends—and even neighbors.

In twenty-three years of observing Bill in action at the office and at Stepping Stones, I saw him counsel innumerable people. He was always a sympathetic listener in these circumstances, a true counselor to AA friends and others, not only with their alcoholic problems but with their personal problems, as well. He always gave them pragmatic answers, not lofty, theoretical opinions. He was compassionate, understanding, and caring.

Though his education stressed engineering and science, he was innately articulate. In his talks, he had a natural eloquence; and in his writings, he had the gift of finding the word that expressed exactly what he wanted to convey. Though not necessarily scholarly, he was knowledgeable and well read, and his choice of language was apt and to the point. When we were working on articles or chapters of a book—or even important, topical letters that might be "for the record"—they usually went through several drafts, each heavily edited by himself. Tom P., a friend and superb writer and speaker himself, openly admired this quality in Bill's work. Bill asked him to edit, over many years, several of his manuscripts before publication—specifically *Twelve Steps and Twelve Traditions* and *AA Comes of Age*. Tom seldom changed his words, concentrating instead on the flow of the thought, sentence structure, and paragraphing.

Bill had a wonderful sense of humor. He was a great storyteller. But he was not much interested in current jokes making the rounds. On many occasions, I watched as friends attempted to share jokes of this kind with him. When the storyteller delivered the punch line, Bill would just stare at him blankly, not reacting in any way, to the chagrin of the storyteller.

Bill loved to tell Vermont stories in authentic dialect. (He didn't have a noticeable accent in his normal speech—unlike Dr. Bob, who was unmistakably a Vermonter.) Regaling us with these stories or relating drunken episodes of his own or others, describing physical characteristics and foibles of early Vermont friends and neighbors, he would not just amuse us, he would send us into gales of laughter, almost falling off our chairs.

AA meetings are full of laughter, which sometimes surprises and shocks the uninitiated. Both Bill and Lois enjoyed and joined in the general mirth. One time at the office, Bill couldn't find a precious document and suggested our office manager, Marian, must have lost it. Marian indignantly denied it, but Bill kept nagging her. Finally he found the paper in a drawer in his own desk. Embarrassed now, he dropped down on all fours and crawled out to Marian's desk with the document in his teeth to beg her forgiveness.

In this instance he was mocking himself, but he did possess genuine humility. He was unfailingly self-depreciating. Underneath, he had a healthy ego, but who doesn't? It was a factor in his successful leadership of A A. But he kept it pretty well reined in. His efforts to push off credit to other people was one way of doing this. His constant, insistent efforts to relinquish his own power as a founder was another evidence of his humility. In the early 1960s, following the appearance of a scathingly critical appraisal of A A in an article by Arthur Cain in *Harper's* magazine, Bill wrote a piece for the *Grapevine* entitled, "Our Critics Can Be Our Benefactors." Hardly the reaction of an egotist. I personally think that people's perception of Bill's ego in the early days arose from his continuous and persistent effort to convince the trustees and members to support the structure and vision he had for the fellowship. This false perception was not helped when Bill himself talked about his ego and his power-driving tendencies. But I feel he often magnified these tendencies to make people feel he was "one of the boys."

I've listened many times as Bill explained his own view of humility. According to him, we need to follow the Greek "middle way"—to strike a balance. We should neither wear the Uriah Heep cloak of false humility, which Bill called "force-feeding of humble pie," nor stray the other way into pride of material achievements and admiration of one's own importance. Bill's definition of humility was willingness to seek God's will in one's life and then follow it. I'm reminded of a statement I saw once posted on the bulletin board of an alcoholic rehabilitation facility. It read:

"There is but one God, and today you are not him."

That's pretty close to Bill's view of humility.

I don't think of Bill as a saintly figure, looking down from some ethereal height, but as a practical, fallible figure, feet planted firmly on the ground, but looking up, seeking answers to his questions and actions.

I think Bill was essentially nonreligious—which may seem paradoxical, because he was deeply spiritual. His whole life was changed by a profound religious experience. The Oxford Group, which was responsible for his early sobriety, was regarded as a religious movement, though their concept of a Higher Power left a lot of latitude for personal interpretation. I have already mentioned Bill's affection for and reliance on his "spiritual sponsor," Father Ed Dowling. About the time I came to the office, he was taking instruction in the Roman Catholic faith regularly with the well-known Monsignor Fulton Sheen. (He never did convert to Catholicism; Lois told me he really hadn't intended to.) And he was pleased when disillusioned and disbelieving alcoholics, as a result of recovering in AA, returned to active church affiliation. Yet for all this deep interest in varieties of spiritual beliefs, Bill was not a churchgoer and all his life avoided joining any particular denomination. I well remember, during our reviewing a draft of *AA Comes of Age*, he suddenly decided to add the following explanation as a footnote to page 232 to clarify his feeling that AA need not and should not endorse any particular religious faith or denomination. He wrote:

> Dr. Bob held certain religious convictions, and so do I. . . . Nothing, however, could be so unfortunate for A.A.'s future as an attempt to incorporate any of our personal theological views into A.A. teaching, practice or tradition.

That was probably part of his motive, but from lots of our talks, I believe it was deeper than that. He was open to all spiritual thinking and did not want to confine himself to one interpretation or one creed. His outlook was probably affected by reading *This Believing World*, by Lewis Browne, which was popular with many AAs—and which influenced my thinking too. As Bill expressed it once to me, he "shopped the pie counter" of religion and philosophy.

In his politics, Bill was a rock-ribbed Vermont conservative. I was a liberal and still am, I guess. We argued a lot at election time until I finally learned to keep my mouth shut. I got weary of arguing and listening to him expound his political views. Like most people on this subject, he was stubborn and wouldn't yield an inch. In his drinking days, he had written fiery letters to President Franklin Roosevelt.

In the fifties, Bill felt that Adlai Stevenson, the Democratic candidate for president, was almost a traitor because he suggested that nuclear bomb testing around certain islands in the Pacific Ocean should be curtailed (an action that was taken not too long afterward). Of course I favored Stevenson for president. One night when Adlai was speaking on television, every time he made a statement Bill didn't agree with (which was most of them), Bill would frown and glance over at me disapprovingly—as if I were responsible. When Lois had had enough of this, she went on to bed; I had to stay up and listen! At the breakfast table the next morning, Bill would put his arm around my shoulders and apologize. He would say something like, "Oh, Nell, we treat you so badly."

He was intellectual and philosophical. He communicated for many years and shared easily with such fine minds as philosophers Gerald Heard and Aldous Huxley, who sincerely admired Bill and openly expressed it. You can see how in the Steps, Traditions, and Concepts Bill considered ideas, conceptual threads, and choices of action from diverse sources before zeroing in on the workable solution, the right choices for AA. He was able to bring together several different streams of thought to form new concepts. For example, the Oxford Group principles, William James's *The Varieties of Religious Experience,* and the Reverend Sam Shoemaker's insights all contributed to the Twelve Steps, but it took Bill (with his own experience added) to meld them into a set of principles, applicable to the alcoholic—and, as it turns out, to every other human ill imaginable.

He also had an unusual faculty for compressing thoughts. For example, at the suggestion of Earl T., founder of AA in Chicago, Bill first wrote essays about the Traditions. These first appeared in the *Grapevine* in 1946–48. He introduced each with the Long Form of the Tradition (found in the back of the Big Book), and later (1949) compressed them into the Short Form of the Twelve Traditions as we know them today. As I said, I watched these metamorphoses happen during my first years at the AA office.

Bill appeared to be easygoing, "laid back" in modern parlance. He spoke with a sort of drawl. And I retain a vivid picture of him at home, even with company present, sprawled out over the floor register. Akron AAs attested to his favorite lounging area at the Smiths' being the living room floor. Dennis Manders remembers him at a drawn-out session of a General Service Conference, stretched out on the carpeted floor at the rear of the meeting room, napping. (I don't remember that!) But when it came to what he thought was necessary and good for the future of the fellowship—such as the General Service Conference idea (to provide a solid structure face and so he could step down from leadership, confident of the stability of the whole fellowship), and the ratio change on the Board of Trustees—he was relentlessly goal-minded, tunnel-visioned, and determined in his efforts to get his proposals understood and accepted. After he had proposed the structuring of AA with the focal point to be a General Service Conference, he didn't receive much encouragement from either the trustees or the membership for a long time. As I said earlier, he believed the trustees were trying to place him in an ivory tower, where he would simply work on writing projects and refrain from stirring up unrest among the groups. But this only made him more determined. So he went out and stumped the United States and Canada in the late forties, explaining and cajoling his listeners to convince them of the need to approve his proposals for the continuity of the fellowship after he and Dr. Bob were gone.

In 1950, there was even a small faction of members long unsympathetic to Bill who, feeling he had "succumbed to madness," contacted the membership themselves to drum up opposition to the conference idea. They called themselves "The Orthodox Group." But they were rebuffed in their attempt to portray Bill as a madman! And, of course at their fall 1950 meeting, the trustees did approve the conference, on a trial basis.

Bill showed the same stubbornness and persistence in his long effort, lasting nearly eleven years, to get the ratio of the General Service Board changed to provide for a majority of alcoholic trustees. The old Alcoholic Foundation, set up in 1939, had originally consisted of five members, three of them nonalcoholics (Rockefeller's friends) to ensure responsibility and continuity of the board in the earliest days when the sobriety of the alcoholics was by no means certain. The board's structure was changed and enlarged in 1943. By 1955 it numbered fifteen, eight of whom were still nonalcoholics (or Class A) and seven who were alcoholics (Class B). Bill began to feel the time had come to change this ratio and set about trying to get it changed. Going through a file from that period, I came across a 1958 letter from Bill to nonalcoholic trustee Harrison Trice, giving his reasons:

- increased press of work with which we have no business to saddle the nonalcoholic members
- proper determination of AA policy and its administration, which the nonalcoholics have disclaimed ability to handle
- need for wider representation geographically of alcoholic trustees
- psychological unsoundness for a movement of our present size and maturity to take a childish and fearful view that a majority of alcoholics cannot be trusted to sit on our most important board

These points specifically and his proposal generally were debated endlessly by the trustees and wrangled over by the delegates at ten conferences, as Bill doggedly pursued his goal. The paradox was that the membership, acting through their delegates, was more opposed to the ratio change than the trustees. Year after year, Bill's proposal was tabled or the decision was passed along to the next conference, until it finally came to a crucial vote in 1962.

One triumph for Bill at that conference was its approval by acclamation of his *Twelve Concepts for World Service.* They did, however, vote down his recommendations, which today still remain in the archive files, untouched.

But the debate that year on his proposed ratio change was long and ornery. The conference again postponed action on it. Immediately following the vote, they adjourned or took a break. During this, few or none of the delegates came up to Bill, who was sitting alone, to support or offer company. As I looked at him across the room, my heart went out to him. I never saw him look so dejected and defeated.

But fortunately, the rejection didn't discourage him for long. At the conferences that followed, he went right back to

buttonholing delegates, explaining and persuading. In fact, Dr.
Jack, Chair of the Board, says that the delegates were reacting
negatively not so much to the idea of the ratio change as to
Bill's tactics in pressuring them. Finally, in 1966 the conference
recommended "that the Board be increased to 21, seven nonalcoholic and 14 alcoholic." And the trustees unanimously accepted the recommendation. Bill was overjoyed at the victory,
but characteristically he shared the credit quite rightly with Dr.
Jack and especially with Herb M. in letters to each of them. His
letter to Herb read in part:

> Without your good offices, your skill and your good will,
> nothing might have been accomplished. . . . I know that AA
> of the future is going to be very greatly in debt to you for this
> contribution . . . during a difficult time in our "pilgrim's
> progress."

I cannot fully tell you what Bill was like without dealing with
his depression. It was such a big part of his life, from his school
days on. It was particularly troublesome during the decade
1945–55. Paradoxically, this was also one of the most produc-
tive decades of his life, as I mentioned before. But it was also a
painful and difficult time for him. It always puzzled him why he
had to endure this suffering since, as he often said, he was so
fortunate and had so much to live for. Since it was obviously not
a mental or attitudinal problem, he felt it must be biochemical.
Interestingly, this conclusion was substantiated in the fifties by
medical, psychiatric, and scientific opinion. He described his
depressive episodes as manic-depressive; it did seem to be true
that his most crippling depressions followed periods of intense
emotional and physical activity, when he was expending enormous amounts of psychic and spiritual energy.

All of us close to Bill—Lois, Dr. Jack, Herb M., myself, and
other friends—were concerned. But outsiders were often less

sympathetic. I witnessed how much criticism he received from some AA members who would suggest somewhat caustically that if he got to meetings and followed his own Twelve Steps, he would be out of trouble. Bill agreed! I can testify that he not only tried valiantly to do just that (he took his Fifth Step with his spiritual sponsor, Father Ed Dowling), but he also sought help from every other avenue he could think of. He saw Dr. Harry Tiebout for psychiatric treatment for a time. He wrote a friend later that it "helped a good deal with my understanding, but I didn't find it curative. It took down my fear [of the depressions], but . . . was not enough to fully overcome them." He had hoped that relief from depression would result from his sessions with Monsignor Fulton Sheen. He found some temporary relief from osteopathic treatments but concluded it wasn't a cure but "just a blowout patch." His "home remedy," as I have mentioned, was concentration on walking—putting one foot in front of the other—and deep breathing. "I had to beat myself to do even this much," he said later.

In the middle 1950s, Bill's friend Gerald Heard introduced him to two English psychiatrists, Dr. Humphrey Osmond and Dr. Abram Hoffer, who were working with schizophrenic and alcoholic patients at a Canadian hospital. They were experimenting with a synthetic chemical called lysergic acid diethylamide—later, in the sixties, notorious as the street drug LSD. But in 1954 there were no laws or regulations governing its usage. The psychiatrists reported it was producing some beneficial effects, being 10 percent more effective than AA help, actually, in their patients, particularly in shortening their resistance to treatment. Bill became enthusiastic about the potential, saying "Anything that helps alcoholics is good and shouldn't be dismissed out of hand." That was typical of his openness to new ideas and therapy. Along with Gerald Heard, he took some of the chemical under the direction of a psychiatrist in California. Returning home, he continued to experiment with it. I tried some myself, as did Lois and other friends. Bill followed closely the scientific results of administering LSD to mental patients and alcoholics over the next two or three years. He withdrew from the experiments completely by 1959 when it was apparent that the whole idea was inconsistent with his position as a founder and "father image" in AA.

Bill continued his friendship with Hoffer and Osmond, however, closely following their work. In the early 1960s they reported they were having some success in treating alcoholics and other victims of depression with massive doses of vitamin B3, also called niacin. Bill had tried the vitamin himself and found, to his joy, that it helped him greatly. In fact, he told me it was the first time in his life he was experiencing life as a normal person must feel it. As Bill became excited about niacin, he shared his enthusiasm with doctor friends in AA and much more widely with AA members, depression being a common condition of alcoholics. He put together three papers about vitamin B3 to help spread the word.

All this caused a big flap among many in the fellowship. Members and trustees alike spoke out against what they viewed as Bill's "using AA" to promote this new, personal "cause" of his. It was true that niacin advocates began voicing their enthusiasm at AA meetings, while those opposed to it used the meetings as a forum to express their views. So it was evident that Bill, without intending to, was violating two of his own Traditions: the Sixth, that AA ought never endorse or lend its name to an outside enterprise; and the Tenth, that AA has no opinion on outside issues, hence the AA name ought never be brought into public controversy. So the Board of Trustees' recommendation was approved at the 1967 conference that all inquiries and activities relating to vitamin B3 should be handled outside of G.S.O. by a separate office using separate stationery. They also recommended using a separate secretary.

I was somewhat resentful of all this fuss. My loyalty was with Bill, and I knew from briefly taking niacin myself and from our correspondence with a large number of AA members that it really had beneficial effects. Bill and Lois too continued to take niacin the rest of their life (Lois, up to a year before she died). Bill kept sharing his enthusiasm with others. I have heard so many AA visitors come up to Bill and thank him for saving their lives twice. After Bill passed away and during the years since then, both Lois and I continued to receive calls and letters asking about Bill's experience in relieving depression by taking niacin. I always share what I can from Bill's experience as did Lois, and from his B3 papers. Lois and I often received their heartfelt thanks in return.

Bill was extraordinarily open-minded and inquisitive. He was a seeker, a searcher. Appropriately, he had a long-time fascination with psychic phenomena, perhaps inevitably because he was rather psychic himself. This was also in keeping with his absolute faith in afterlife. Dr. Bob and Anne S. were also interested in psychic phenomena. In the early forties Bill and Lois often held seances—or "spook sessions" as they termed them—in a small downstairs bedroom at Stepping Stones, which ever after Lois called the "spook room." AA friends, a couple of Rockefeller people, and even some Bedford Hills neighbors frequently participated in these sessions and experienced unusual phenomena. One evening with the Reverend Willard Richardson present, Bill spelled out alphabetically a paragraph or two (in Latin, as it turned out) from a sermon by St. Boniface, verified by Reverend Richardson, also a Latin scholar. Bill had only a vague idea who St. Boniface was and had never read any sermon of his in English—to say nothing of Latin.

One of Bill's most astonishing and convincing experiences took place during a 1947 visit (Bill and Lois's first) to Nantucket Island. They arrived at night. Bill rose early the next morning. While sitting alone in his host's kitchen over a cup of coffee, he heard a lengthy conversation between several persons who had lived more than a hundred years before: among them, a long-dead whaler, a sailor who said his name was David Morrow, who had been killed serving under Admiral Farragut at the Battle of Mobile Bay; and a sea captain named Pettingill. "Just for fun, I told this story at breakfast," Bill wrote later, "making such pointed reference to the names." Their host was skeptical, to say the least, and the matter was dropped.

The next day, Bill, Lois, and their hosts were meeting others for a picnic, rendezvousing at the head of Nantucket's main street. At that spot was a small monument to Nantucket's fallen in the Civil War, at the foot of which were chiseled the names of the dead. One of them was David Morrow! Bill called his host's attention to it. The next day, they visited the Nantucket Whaling Museum for the first time. There in an open book were the names of masters of the old whaling vessels. One of them was Pettingill! "There isn't even a remote chance that I had at some time read or heard about [these] ordinary former inhabitants of the island," Bill wrote. "Maybe one, but certainly not [more than that]."

In the 1950s, Duke University became the center of experiments in precognition. They assembled extensive records of extrasensory perceptions. Bill had some correspondence with Dr. J. B. Rhine of Duke in regard to these, as well as with other investigators in this field.

As might be expected from his military service, Bill was patriotic. He loved his country—and he was loyal all his life to his native Vermont. Bill returned several times a year—and Lois often drove up with him in their Jeep. They stayed at the Londonderry Inn or the Equinox Hotel in Manchester. They walked a lot, talked a lot, and worked a lot on their separate writing projects for AA and Al-Anon. They also liked to stay at these and other "hideaways" near home for a day or two at a time, away from telephone calls and visitors. Occasionally I accompanied them too. Bill also shared with and counseled lots of people: AAs, Al-Anons, and others whom they had simply come to know, such as the owners of the hotels. Later, as I obtained histories from these hotel proprietors, they told me that Bill had made helpful suggestions to them regarding depression or other problems. Bill returned home from these trips refreshed, ready to do battle again with the trustees. He would bring back drafts of memos and *Grapevine* articles ready for me to type. And he would usually bring back some of those wonderful Vermont stories to share with us.

My own first visit to Vermont was with Bill and Lois in the fall of 1960. The occasion was the twenty-fifth anniversary of AA in Vermont. The place was Burlington. Bill and Lois were the guests of honor of course, and Dr. Bob and Anne were honored in absentia, as Vermont was also Dr. Bob's home state. Bill and Bob received a citation from Governor Robert Stafford. I enjoyed attending some of the Al-Anon meetings as well as the AA meetings and was terribly impressed with the spouses' stories, tribulations, and contributions and came to admire them and their work as much as that of AA's. In the AA Archives, we have tapes of that great weekend.

The occasion of my second visit to Vermont was Bill's burial and memorial service in East Dorset on May 8, 1971. Lois's brother, Rogers (who had introduced her to Bill), had died in December 1970—about a month before Bill. He was interred around the same time as Bill but in another nearby cemetery. Lois visited Rogers's gravesite too of course. Dr. Jack and his wife, Ellie, attended Bill's service also.

Again, in February 1984, I drove up with Lois's and my friend, Joan B., from Toronto, to visit Bill's sister and brother-in-law, Dorothy and Leonard Strong. On the same trip I gathered some oral histories for the archives in the East Dorset-Arlington-Manchester area and, with Orlando and Dorothy C., visited historic sites such as the cemetery where Bill and family members were buried, Rowland H.'s home (one-story, rambling but picturesque, set in the lovely, hilly countryside), Bill and Ebby's school, Burr and Burton Seminary, and the grandparents' house where Bill grew up.

During this visit, accompanied by Orlando C., I also visited Manchester airport, the site of one of Bill's more famous drunken adventures. The year was 1929. Bill and Ebby had been partying all night in Albany with another drinking friend, a pilot, Ted Burke. A daring scheme managed to penetrate the alcoholic fog: to fly to Manchester the next day in Ted's small plane. The Manchester airport was just being completed but had not yet been used. At some point the pilot called ahead to the Manchester flight center to announce their imminent arrival. The story goes that the excited Manchester folks got together a welcoming committee and the town band; the delegation was headed by Mrs. Anna Simonds Orvis, the dignified owner of the famous Equinox House.

Bill told later that the three of them in the plane had been "pulling at a bottle" on the way up.

> We circled the field and somehow lit on the pretty bumpy meadow. The [welcoming] delegation charged forward. It was up to Ebby and me to do something. . . . We somehow slid out of the cockpit, fell on the ground, and there we lay, immobile. Such was the history-making episode of the first airplane ever to light at Manchester, Vermont.

But more than fifty years later, at the scene itself, here we were, standing at the gate of that silent, long-abandoned airport, the wind gently swaying the tall, soft weeds on the field, revealing the old landing-wheel patterns of the incoming planes. The still in-position sign on the fence entrance faced us, warning that all intruders on the field without permission would be prosecuted for interfering with operations of the airfield. It bought an eerie feeling of nostalgia, as I tried to mentally reconstruct that incredible scene that even today many townspeople still remember and talk about.

In the last few years, I have returned to the beautiful state of Vermont several more times. On October 10, 1988, we held a small family burial service at Lois's gravesite, right beside Bill. Recently it was a pleasure to attend Founders Day in East Dorset, during which a moving memorial service was held at the gravesite of Bill and Lois. At least 150 people were present, with cars lined along both sides of the highway for a long way on either side of the cemetery entrance.

That both cofounders of Alcoholics Anonymous came from Vermont is one of those AA "coincidences" that had an unknown but significant role in the founding and survival of Alcoholics Anonymous. Their love of their native Vermont was not the only thing they shared, as I'll tell you in the next chapter.

Nell Wing conducting research for *Grateful to Have Been There.*

8

Bill and Dr. Bob

*T*HE MEETING IN MAY 1935 of the to-be cofounders of Alcoholics Anonymous, their immediate rapport, and the wonderfully close and supportive relationship that lasted until Dr. Bob's death in November 16, 1950, has always seemed to me a genuine miracle. One side of the miracle was that they shared so many things in common. Had they not, there might never have been an AA! The other side of the miracle was the many contrasts and differences in the two men; they complemented each other perfectly. I truly believe that no other combination of men would have worked.

Occasionally—more often in the early days than recently—I would hear a loyal Akronite say that it was Bob who made the most impact, who held the fellowship together and saved it from Bill's ego and wild schemes—or from an Eastern member, that it was Bill's efforts at unification that kept AA intact. That always disturbed me a bit because it represents a serious misinterpretation of the miracle as I saw it. It wasn't a question of one being more important than the other; they made two parts of a whole. Dr. Bob, in Bill's phrase, was the "fisher of men" (though Bill did his share too), while Bill (as Bernard Smith once called him) was "the architect of the fellowship," the builder of the house AA lived in. The beautiful and workable part was their devotion to each other and their deep respect for the other's opinions and contributions to each other and the fellowship. Bill often described Bob as "the rock upon which AA was founded."

I am often asked if I knew Dr. Bob. Regrettably, I saw him only once, and that briefly. It was in the fall of 1948, when he joined Bill and Lois at the annual Intergroup Dinner in New York, one of the rare appearances of the two men together. Dr. Bob also came into the office. Our small office was packed like a sardine can that day for this occasion. I was on duty as the receptionist switchboard operator. I had left the room on an errand, because the picture I have in my memory is of this tall, husky, slightly stooped man leaving the reception area. So my only clear memory of him is from the rear! However, I feel I know both Dr. Bob and Anne very well indeed through Bill and Lois's descriptive personal memories of them—and other AA friends sharing anecdotes about them, via oral history tapes for the archives over the years.

Isn't it incredible that when these two alcoholics who so desperately needed each other were brought together out in Akron, they discovered they were both Vermonters? They shared a common New England heritage. Also when they first talked that Sunday in Akron, Bill, refraining from the impulse to "preach," laid heavy emphasis on the medical aspects of alcoholism that he had learned from Dr. William Silkworth; and Bob, as a physician himself, was receptive to the message.

Dr. Bob became, as Bill described him, "the prince of the Twelfth Steppers"—a title for which he was well qualified, growing out of his natural instinct as a doctor for helping people, combined with his intense desire as an alcoholic to administer to his fellow sufferers. He was also cautious by nature, not given to hasty opinions, down to earth, used to certain discipline, patient, practical, sure of himself on professional terms—more influenced by, and a listener to, the ideas of others, less willing to take a chance and thereby risk a mistake. Bob often urged caution on Bill as well. Although he shared Bill's vision of AA's future, he felt no action should be taken until complete agreement on any suggested proposal had been secured in advance. Though he didn't always agree with the timing of Bill's projects and proposals, he always backed him up—out of deep loyalty and affection.

Bill, on the other hand, reflecting his Wall Street training perhaps, was always thinking ahead. He possessed a natural talent for seeing needs down the road. An activist, good writer, and charismatic speaker, he felt that any innovative step or action for the better functioning of the fellowship in the future should be tried. If it didn't work, it could be dropped; but the effort should be made. I've heard him say many times that one must try to aim for a goal. A person won't be faulted for failing to achieve it, only for failing to try hard enough.

The temperaments and personalities of the two cofounders differed. Bob appeared to be shyer in public appearances than Bill, but in private he was more gregarious, according to friends. He was always one of the crowd, enjoying getting off with his buddies and relaxing. He liked to spend time fishing at the lakeside. I remember a picture of him, with a friend on one side and a propped-up fish, which looked a head taller than either of them, on the other side, and wide, happy grins on their faces—except on the fish of course. He liked to play cards and watch fights on early television; he liked cars and drove them fast. But apparently he didn't desire or totally enjoy speaking at large gatherings. Bill was just the opposite. He was a more private man who often felt awkward and ill at ease in small social situations; but he was sure of himself in public and enjoyed sharing and speaking to large or small crowds, usually at conferences and conventions. It became difficult, in his position, to visit individual groups. He had planned, before the 1955 anniversary convention in St. Louis, to visit several groups to explain in more detail his reasons and plans for relinquishing leadership. But other groups protested vigorously and demanded he visit them also—so he had to cancel the original visiting plan entirely.

Right from the beginning of their relationship, Bill and Bob felt close and protective of each other—even though they were widely separated by distance for long periods of time. Bob worried about Bill's health, and Bill worried about Bob's money situation, a mortgage on the house, for example. (Dr. Bob was spending so much time treating alcoholics, for which he would take no compensation, that his regular practice had all but dried up.) Bill, in partnership with Hank P., had formed Works Publishing Company in early 1939 to publish the Big Book. At Bill's insistence, a major condition of their turning over their interest in Works Publishing to the Alcoholic Foundation in 1940 was that Bob and Anne would receive a royalty on the Big Book for the rest of their lives. Bob, however, was mindful of Bill and Lois's own unsteady financial condition and insisted that Bill should take some part of Bob's royalty when he needed it. The matter was somewhat academic anyway, because for the first year or two the Big Book wasn't selling well, so neither of them received royalties. After that discouraging period, however, the book started to sell, and when the book debts were repaid, both Bill and Bob received royalties from the foundation, Bob's being made retroactive to 1940.

Bill made an effort on his own in 1939 to obtain financial relief for Bob by requesting a grant from the Guggenheim Foundation in New York. He wrote in part:

At Akron, Ohio, there is a physician, Dr. Robert H. S——, who has been responsible during the last four years for the recovery of at least 100 chronic alcoholics of types hitherto regarded by the medical profession as hopeless . . . without charge to sufferers, without fanfare and almost without funds. . . .

Because of his great amount of voluntary alcoholic work, the doctor has been unable to rebuild his surgical practice.

If he continues [alcoholic] work at the present pace, he may lose the remainder of his practice and probably his home. Obviously, he should continue, but how?

Bill then suggested a stipend of three thousand dollars for one year, reassuring the Guggenheim that other efforts were being made to provide necessary funds. He closed the letter with the words, "He knows nothing of this approach on his behalf."

The Guggenheim Foundation replied, holding out little hope of being able to accommodate Dr. Bob, since their fellowships were given to creative and original works in the arts. Bill was sufficiently discouraged that he let the matter drop.

Both Bill and Bob shared a rollicking sense of humor. They loved to tease. They liked to tell stories (not jokes, but stories), and they were both good at it. Bob was noted for using little parables to make his points with those he was helping. They both enjoyed giving people nicknames—including each other. Bill almost always called Bob "Doc" or "Smith." Dr. Bob called Bill "Willie" or "Sir William." Occasionally, in Bob's letters to Ruth Hock at the office, Bill was simply "that guy," as in "Tell that guy to write when you see him." (Bill wasn't always the best correspondent in the world.)

I don't know whether it was because Bill and Dr. Bob were Vermonters or because of the era in which they grew up, but both of them used quaint, amusing expressions. Bob would have been the despair of today's feminists, for to him, a woman was a "frail," a ring was a "rock." When Bill was ready to take a walk with Lois he'd say, "Let's take a tunk." (I can't imagine where that one came from, nor could Lois.) When a debate or an argument was coming to a climax, it was "hotting up." I've already mentioned one of his favorite sayings, "hold fast"— meaning stay with it, hang in there. If he wasn't feeling up to par, he was "cooking up soggy."

The turbulent early days of AA had their share of setbacks and disappointments, for which Bill had a variety of expressions. On hearing of disagreements in groups or between people, he would say in a mock rural Vermont accent, "Hit's the people!" or a variation on that. For example, if a member had an alcoholic slip, Bill might say, "Oh, the people, they won't stay fixed." Or, if someone broke his anonymity or a squabble broke out in a clubhouse, Bill would say, "That's life among the Anonymii!" Starting a meal, Bill would say "How we eat it." On finishing a meal, Bill would take his glass and land it firmly on the table—a New England custom, apparently.

One amazing "coincidence" in Bill and Dr. Bob's initial meeting, which was surely a profound influence in the firm rapport they established, was that they had both been involved in the Oxford Group—Bill, in the months after he emerged from Towns Hospital in December 1934; Dr. Bob, seeking help from the Akron Oxford Group on his own, albeit at the urging of his wife, Anne, and Henrietta Seiberling. Therefore, as soon as meetings of alcoholics began to be held in Akron, they followed the Oxford Group format and principles. According to early accounts, Bob and Anne and families of alcoholics would hold the meetings in their homes, morning and evening. Bob, according to several accounts, liked to sit with an open Bible on his lap, out of which a passage would be selected at random and read. A discussion would then follow on its relevance to the personal life problems of those present. The emphasis was on day-to-day living, how to cope with personal problems, and self-examination—though alcoholism as an illness was also discussed. (The recovering alcoholic in those days, on his first contact with the prospect, typically shared his own story in the hospital, to establish identification, and I imagine, to contact the alcoholic at his bottom point!) Guidance (an Oxford Group expression) was nearly always asked for and listened to. (AA's use of the word *sharing* was also a frequently used Oxford Group expression.) *Witnessing* was another word—similar to sharing.

Dr. Bob, as any well-disciplined doctor, could be firm with the hospitalized patient—establishing up front if the alcoholic wanted outside help—something other than medical assistance. Any response less than a positive one brought an immediate negative reaction from Bob—"Come back when you're ready" or something similar. But if the alcoholic patient expressed willingness to be helped, over and above his physical needs, Bob and the small handful of members responded immediately and caringly with AA's message.

Somewhere around the end of 1936 or early 1937, the alcoholics' meetings outgrew the relatively modest homes of Bob and Anne and their friends, so they began meeting at the home of T. Henry and Clarace Williams, who headed up the Oxford Group in Akron.

Apparently, the "alcoholic squad" met separately from the regular Oxford Groupers, though both groups opened and closed the meeting jointly. Before joining the meeting of the alcoholic squad (also called while still associated with the local Oxford Group "First Century Christian Fellowship"), a newcomer was asked (as Bob did in hospitalizing a prospective member) if he wanted to make a surrender, a first and crucial decision. If the answer was yes, the new man was taken upstairs by Dr. Bob or a couple of other members. The surrender was made on his knees, and they all came back downstairs, the newcomer usually pale and shaken. (One wife was reported being visibly alarmed, as she watched her husband wobble unsteadily down the stairs!) Reflecting this Oxford Group experience, Bill, in the first draft of the Twelve Steps, began Step Seven, "Humbly, on our knees . . ." And Ruth Hock tells of coming to work for Bill and Hank P. at the Honor Dealers office on William Street in Newark. She was not too clear herself as to the nature of the business and was astonished one day, early in her employment, to glimpse in Hank and Bill's office a visitor on his knees beside the desk with Bill and Hank bending over, talking earnestly to him.

Returning home the later part of August 1935 after spending the summer in Dr. Bob and Anne's home, Bill continued to attend Oxford Group meetings in New York. However, single-minded though he was in his concern for alcoholics and the application of the Oxford Group principles in their staying sober, he was not interested in the Oxford Group's zeal to save the world. Nor was the Oxford Group, according to its founder, Frank Buchman, interested in saving all the alcoholics in the world! Therefore, the alcoholics in New York came to a parting of the ways with the Oxford Group at Calvary Episcopal Church in 1937, two years before the break was made in Akron. Years later, having heard Bill acknowledge many times the debt that AA owed to the Oxford Group, the Reverend Sam Shoemaker wrote him a moving and humble letter that read in part:

> Bill, if you ever write the story of AA's early connection with Calvary [Church], I think it ought to be said in all honesty we were coached in the feeling that you were off on your own spur, trying to do something by yourself, and out of the mainstream of the OG work. I remember very well. You got your

inspiration from those early days, but you didn't get much encouragement from any of us. . . . Fortunately, it didn't keep you from going on and beginning this amazing contribution to one of the vast needs of this day.

In this, I feel Dr. Shoemaker was overmodest, for through Bill his influence on the AA program was enormous. He became and remained a close, special friend of Bill and all AA members until his death in October 1963.

Bob and Bill shared that unique and priceless gift to AA of avoidance of power or position. Neither of them wanted to be regarded as a spiritual leader removed from a society of followers. Both of them rejected any attempt to put them on a pedestal. Each of them truly thought of himself as "just another drunk." With Bill at many large gatherings as well as in the office, I have seen so many members over the years, from all parts of the world, rush up to him, hug him tightly (to his embarrassment), and pour out their love and gratitude. He would immediately but affectionately turn aside their effusiveness and say, "Pass it on" or perhaps, "Look, I'm just another drunk. Pass it on." (Most appropriately, that expression of Bill's was chosen as the title of AA's biography of its cofounder, *Pass It On*. Incidentally, I've seldom, if ever, heard Bill describe alcoholism as a disease—his most often used phrases were *malady* or *illness*.)

I'd like to share a letter from Bill to Dr. Bob, August 26, 1940. The nostalgia, the spiritual pragmatism, the quality of delight and exultation at the successful start of AA, is so heartwarming, I am moved to tears every time I read it. If there are any special words of Bill's to be treasured forever, celebrating the true perspective of AA's beginnings, this letter says it all.

To say that I am overjoyed with the progress of Alcoholics Anonymous is stating the case mildly. For a long time I was

fearful that weak situations . . . would develop in large num-
bers as a result of publicity and half-baked starts. But even
Washington now has a strong group and places that were
shaky such as Los Angeles and San Francisco are coming on
beautifully both in quality and quantity. It has become evident only with the last two or three months that the casual
traveler, the book, and our central office correspondence
and "propaganda" is sufficient to spread AA all over the
country. That is a demonstrated fact about which I have no
doubt whatever. Neither would anyone who has seen the
amazing correspondence which rolls into this office. In some
instances there has been no personal contact at all—just our
correspondence and the book. An increasing number of people are coming to light who have been dry on the book alone.
In many instances they have commenced to work with other
people. It is all truly miraculous. Considering the amount of
attention and nursing and the great difficulty of starting the
original groups, it is all quite incomprehensible. Nevertheless, nationwide success is already here. We cannot possibly
fail now.

Alcoholics Anonymous was so fortunate and blessed in its
cofounders. One wonders what the outcome of other societies
popular in the last few decades might have been if their failed
founders had adhered to the same spiritual principles as did
AA's leaders (along with the rest of the fellowship): seeking
and practicing genuine humility in all one's affairs; placing
principles before personalities; maintaining one-on-one peer
relationships with the newcomer; sharing together with rigor-
ous honesty; growing in maturity and spiritual enlightenment;
and in the end, demonstrating an eagerness to step down from
leadership rather than trying to hang onto it.

Finally, Dr. Bob and Bill died and were buried with the same
humility they had shown in their lifetimes. Shortly before Dr.

Bob's death, Akron AA's proposed to honor him with an imposing mausoleum and monument. When he saw the plans and had shown them to Bill, he drawled, "I reckon we ought to be buried like other folks." Bill agreed emphatically. And so they were, both of them. Except for obituaries in the papers, in which their anonymity was broken, there was little fanfare. Their tombstones make no mention of AA. Although memorial services were held by AAs throughout the nation and the world, only old friends and relatives attended their actual funeral services. Aside from June 10, 1935, Bob's sobriety date—which has been designated to mark the beginning of AA history—no other significant dates in their lives are celebrated or observed—no birthdays, nor sobriety dates, nor dates of deaths. And I'm sure that few AA members could name any of these. Which is just as Bill and Bob would have wanted it.

The same care for personal privacy was observed at Lois's burial service on October 10, 1988, at East Dorset, where she now rests beside her beloved Bill. And I'm sure this was equally true at Anne's service in June 1949 in Akron.

Through the constantly recurring miracle of Alcoholics Anonymous, the contributions of the cofounders live on, in a direct, unbroken chain, in the sobriety and the daily lives of millions of AA members throughout the world today. That was all they wanted to leave behind.

9

Bill and Dr. Bob: Postscript

*I*MMERSED THOUGH I WAS in the absorbing and exciting world of Alcoholics Anonymous, I shared to some extent the members' awe of their cofounders. I never tired of hearing Bill tell about his telephone call for help to Henrietta Seiberling, who put him in touch with Dr. Bob on that fateful Saturday in Akron, and how he and Dr. Bob finally met the next afternoon at the Seiberling gatehouse. When I eventually became the AA archivist, I was thrilled to think that sometime I might come across some written documentation of the meeting, something that would give the world new insights into how Bill and Dr. Bob themselves viewed that historic occasion. I felt sure that Bill, with his sense of vision, would have evaluated its importance in an epochal way.

Finally, in the late seventies, I found what I was looking for. It happened on one of my usual weekend visits to Stepping Stones. Lois excitedly asked me to read a newly discovered collection of letters (stowed away years before, down in the cellar) that Bill had written her from Akron during that important summer of 1935. For Lois, the rereading had brought back memories of deep feelings of both happiness and disappointment at that time: happiness that Bill was sober and making friends; disappointment that he did not return as soon as she had expected.

As I read through the missives, my heart commenced to pound when I found in my hand the very letter that Bill had written to Lois on that fateful Mother's Day in May 1935.

He wrote:

"Today I met a man who has my problem."

10

Bill's "Shortcomings and Character Defects"

OVER THE LAST FIFTEEN YEARS or more, I've been invited occasionally to AA area meetings, conferences, and conventions to share my memories of Bill and Lois and the fellowship's incredible early history. After listening to me prattle on at one such gathering about Bill's virtues and contributions, a member came up to me later and asked, "But didn't Bill have any character defects at all?" I was momentarily taken aback, realizing I had perhaps gone overboard on his good points, creating the impression of some divine infallability! So I hastened to reply, "Well, yes, of course he did. After all he was human. Bill wasn't perfect. Who of us is? In fact a longtime AA friend used to say 'he wore his halo a bit on the jaunty side.'"

Before we start, I must say I'm uneasy discussing anyone else's "defects," including Bill's. I guess maybe to most people who were around in the structure-building years especially, his most obvious "character defect"—one he spoke about himself—was his power-driving. Once he got his teeth into an idea or proposal that he considered necessary, good, and practical for AA's successful future operations (like linkage of services, AA's financial security, literature needs, grassroots delegate representation, a strong and secure Board of Trustees and General Service Conference Operations) he seldom let go until he had pushed it through. He could be in some circumstances really tenacious and stubborn, which could and did annoy many people. But that is the only way he was able to accomplish what he did.

Right from the beginning with the writing of the AA book, Bill had to push vigorously for nearly every major proposal or concept to broaden the effectiveness of the AA program and structure, including the Twelve Steps. There was in the early Akron days a preference for keeping the movement small, one-on-one, seeking quality not quantity. (Some early members as shared in their oral histories, perceived it as a sort of "gentlemen's club.") So Bill was always confronting apathy, ultraconservatism, the trustees, or factions within the fellowship who did not agree with his ideas.

When he was trying to convince you in an argument, he was not above a little arm twisting, as many people can attest to. If he felt the issue needed an immediate decision and you still disagreed, he could really pound at you, backing you into a verbal corner until any equanimity you had went up in smoke. As he went on and on, you wanted to retaliate in anger. He was sometimes his own worst enemy, for people often said they reacted not to his ideas but to his strident tactics trying to convince them. Maybe so, but I remember those early days and there really seemed to be a lack of enthusiasm right from the start for many of his suggestions.

A friend and longtime associate at the office, Dennis Manders says (similar to what I said earlier), "Bill was not much for small talk. You carried on a spirited conversation with him as long as you stuck to the subject he was hot on at the moment. If you tried to shift to another subject, he might simply walk away." Yet he could also be a marvelously patient and sympathetic listener to people, including me, who came to him for advice on a variety of subjects. But when he was on one of his "crusades," his eyes and mind were fixed on the goal, and he was impatient to come to decisions as soon as possible, no matter how long it might take to carry them out.

Along with this trait, he was also a dedicated, tireless talker. Many weekends at Stepping Stones with company present, I remember Bill leaning back in a straight chair, arms in motion, holding the conversational floor as he expounded on whatever aspect of AA was currently engaging his attention—the conference, trustee ratio question, or the Concepts. Not many people interrupted him once he got started, including relatives. When Lois tried, he would shoot a slight frown in her direction. When he tried the same tactic with me, I pretended I didn't notice and typically barged right in with my own comments. A family member recalled that holiday visits were too often given over to Bill's long AA monologues. But this was really Bill's way of refining and defining new issues—verbalizing them, noting reactions—before he set them to paper. Of course, this didn't help those who had to sit and listen for long periods of time.

Many members recall Bill's tendency to exaggerate. Ruth Hock remembered that when talking before a meeting, he was prone to be overgenerous in quoting the latest membership count or meetings' attendance. He might say for example, there were 150 members. Ruth, who was quite literal-minded (as I am myself), would lean over and whisper, "No Bill, it's only ninety-five" or whatever the actual figure was in those days. Afterward, Bill would complain good-naturedly, "Oh, Ruth, you're spoiling the fun."

Bill always claimed that the attendance at the 1955 International Convention in St. Louis was five thousand. Dennis, who handled the registrations, told me the true figure was about thirty-one hundred plus possibly a few hundred walk-ins. I do recall myself that the crowd nowhere near filled Kiel Auditorium. This exaggeration stemmed in part from Bill's intense focus on the growth and development of AA, so he was a little ahead in his own mind. For example, the title page of the first edition of Alcoholics Anonymous reads, "The Story of How One Hundred Men Have Recovered from Alcoholism." It is doubtful that there were a hundred continuously sober members when that was written in 1939, though by the following year the figure was already obsolete.

Bill may also have reflected AA's general disregard for statistics then. Because membership in the fellowship is anonymous and no detailed records or statistics were kept of individuals—except correspondence—and also because there are no dues or fees, there are no reliable figures of total membership to this day. So everyone is free to make his or her own guess.

Also, Bill was not always tactful. He was often blunt, straightforward, likely to lay it right on the line. And he sometimes lacked a sense of confidentiality. If you had a secret, it wouldn't do to share it immediately with Bill, who was likely to blurt it out unless you made him raise his right hand and hope to die!

He could appear to be absentminded—consistent with his tunnel vision. He had the classic problem of trying to keep track of his glasses—only to be reminded they rested on top of his head. In 1950 the office moved from 415 Lexington Avenue around the corner to 141 East Forty-Fourth Street. Bill would arrive from upstate Bedford Hills into Grand Central Station on the commuter train. Thinking of weightier matters, he would bound through the station and across Lexington with those long strides of his and head directly into the old building. The elevator operator would hurry over to him saying, "No, no, Mr. W——! You're located around the corner now." This happened not once, but many times.

Bill was somewhat wary of new technology, new techniques. When it was decided to make a home-movie-style of documentary, *Bill's Own Story*, he had a kind of stage fright in front of the camera. As comfortable as he was with words and talking, he felt awkward and uncomfortable in the presence of that unblinking eye and the mikes suspended overhead. I was there at Stepping Stones the day the filming started and remember how Bill fussed, finding all kinds of reasons why a particular scene wouldn't work. However, when they got down to filming, Bill and Lois's lack of professionalism added to the charm. I think this film has been translated into several languages. I remember when Lois and I were attending the Twenty-Fifth AA Anniversary in Switzerland in 1981. We viewed the French version of it—a wonderful experience.

What Bill felt about cameras, he also felt about new dictating machines. Until the end, we were using a pair of antique dictating machines, then about twenty-two years old. They not only were no longer being manufactured, the plastic discs were no longer made either. However, we had a good supply in storage. Bill felt comfortable with them, and I really didn't mind either.

Many interpreted Bill's persistence and power-driving as coming from a large ego. Sure, Bill did have an ego. Who doesn't? What amazed me during the years with Bill, and even more in retrospect, is that someone with such a healthy ego could so successfully suppress it and sublimate it in all his actions: discounting his own contributions, insisting on the co-founder concept, always sharing credit with others, turning down public honors (the Lasker award, the Yale degree), eschewing power and glory, and stepping down from leadership.

Dr. Sam Shoemaker in a letter to Bill summed it up pretty well when he said, "God has saved you from the love of the spotlight, Bill—at least, if not from the love of it, from getting too much into it. It is one of the biggest things about you, and I often speak of it."

To some members, Bill's failure to attend AA meetings regularly was a grievous fault. He even regarded it as such himself. But the fellowship just wouldn't permit this cofounder to attend meetings as an ordinary AA member. That was one of the disappointments of Bill's AA life, for he desperately wanted the healing, the insights, the spiritual renewal that all members find at meetings. He yearned wistfully on occasion to be an anonymous AA member in the back row. But this just didn't become possible, which meant that Bill was always giving, seldom taking. In October 1947 he wrote an article on the subject for the *Grapevine*, "Why Can't We Join AA, Too?" It was in the form of a letter from Dr. Bob and himself addressed to the membership and he explains pretty thoroughly this dilemma of his and Bob's coleadership.

When Bill did drop in at a meeting, he was always asked to speak. He was either lionized or subjected to unsolicited advice about what he should do about certain issues—or both. Of course, at Stepping Stones he was surrounded by AA's and Al-Anons both in person and by phone. And I recall an endless procession of people seeking his personal Twelve Stepping or his advice in their later sobriety—and the endless hours he devoted to them. That's why when I hear or read about AA's saying Bill did not do any Twelfth Step work I bristle. Not so!

11

Influences on Bill

*H*OW COULD BILL HAVE AC-complished all that he did? I've had many people, especially outside the fellowship, ask me that. They express astonishment that any one person, no matter how intelligent or inspired, could have written the Big Book and the other literature and could have devised the Traditions, the AA structure, the Concepts—plus all his other incredible accomplishments—in a relatively short time period while traveling and speaking so extensively. And so much of it done in the middle of painful depressive periods that even members weren't aware of.

A good AA friend said he heard the famous Clancy I. give his own ideas about it in a humorous talk. Clancy is a colorful AA who is invited to do a tremendous amount of AA speaking. He is also known as a hard but extremely successful sponsor of hundreds and hundreds of alcoholics that others had given up on. So he has seen at first hand the length of time required for the growth and development that takes place in a recovering alcoholic. My friend heard Clancy make a talk about the Big Book in which he said, "I'm not a particularly religious person, but I tell you I am absolutely positive that the Big Book had to have been written with Divine Guidance. Because it was written in 1938, when Bill W. was only about two-and-one-half years sober. And if you'll think back on the mental condition of new-comers you have worked with, at two-and-one-half years sober they can hardly put two coherent sentences together. And yet Bill wrote this book, which has been responsible for the recovery of millions of hopeless alcoholics all over the world." Clancy then goes on sardonically, "Why, I would hardly trust a sponsee with ten years' sobriety to make a major decision! And I would hardly leave one with five years' sobriety alone at night! As for one with two-and-a-half years' sobriety, I wouldn't even trust him to go out for coffee! He'd come back after a while with, 'Say, was that two blacks and one regular with sugar—or was it two regulars and one black with sugar?'" The audience howls with glee because there's truth in Clancy's exaggeration.

And then Clancy ends with, "Don't tell me Bill could have written this book without outside help!"

The truth is that Bill was possessed of a special, eclectic type of intelligence. He was a great synthesizer. He had a remarkable ability to take ideas and concepts from many different sources, and then pick the best or the most applicable and combine them into the works that prompt such astonishment in people. He said on many occasions, "Nobody invented AA" or "Everything in AA is borrowed from somewhere else." Although that is an overstatement, Bill did draw from many other sources that influenced him.

First and foremost, he was profoundly influenced by his own spiritual experience in Towns Hospital after what proved to be his last binge. The experience really began with Ebby's earlier visit, when Bill was drinking in the kitchen of his home on Clinton Street, having hardly drawn a sober breath in five years. Up to that time he had been an agnostic. He had believed vaguely in a Power greater than himself, but with ministers and religions, "my mind snapped shut," he said.

> My friend sat before me, and he made the point-blank declaration that God had done for him what he could not do for himself. . . . Doctors had pronounced him incurable. . . . Then he had, in effect, been raised from the dead, suddenly taken from the scrap heap to a level of life better than the best he had ever known! . . . [But] there remained in me the vestiges of my old prejudice. . . . I could go for such conceptions as Creative Intelligence, Universal Mind or Spirit of Nature but I resisted the thought of a Czar of the Heavens, however loving his sway might be. . . .
>
> At the hospital I was separated from alcohol for the last time.

Ebby visited Bill again there and finding him much more receptive, talked earnestly to him about giving up his self-centeredness and believing in the power of God or a Higher Power concept. When his friend left, Bill abandoned himself and cried out, "If there is a God, let Him reveal Himself now!" With that he said the room seemed to fill with light.

> There was a sense of victory, followed by such a peace and serenity as I had never known. . . . I felt lifted up, as though the great clean wind of a mountain top blew through and through. God comes to most men gradually, but His impact on me was sudden and profound.

This story of Bill's not only constitutes the heart of chapter 1 of the Big Book, but he retold it many thousands of times as long as he lived. Without this life-altering spiritual experience, there would have been no recovery and no accomplishments.

A part of this experience was the book *The Varieties of*

Religious Experience, by the psychologist William James. It was, of itself, an important influence on Bill. Ebby is supposed to have brought the book with him to Towns Hospital, where he left it with Bill. It may well have helped prepare Bill for his spiritual experience. In any case, his avid reading of it after the experience greatly widened his spiritual horizons. In it he read about many other people who had had experiences like his own. They were described in scientific, psychological terms, rather than in a religious context. William James dwelt at length on the importance of deflation of ego as a prerequisite to receiving power greater than oneself. Bill had been at the low point of his life when he called on the God he didn't really believe in, and he recognized the special importance of this step for the alcoholic. *The Varieties of Religious Experience* was a major influence on Bill's emphasizing the necessity of deflation of ego in chapter 5 of the Big Book. And note, the First Step is, "We admitted we were powerless over alcohol—that our lives had become unmanageable." James's book not only influenced Bill but also became basic reading for many of the early AA members.

Another seminal influence on Bill—indeed, one of the cornerstones on which the AA program was built—was Dr. William Silkworth, the Medical Director of Towns Hospital. He treated Bill on all three of his trips to Towns and was of immeasurable help to Lois in understanding the illness that gripped her husband. In fact, on Bill's third visit, Dr. Silkworth told Lois that it would probably be his last, that he could not survive another bout of drinking like the one he had just been through. Bill overheard this dismal diagnosis, which may well have contributed to his deflation of ego and perhaps helped prepare him for his mountaintop spiritual experience a bit later.

Dr. Silkworth was a man of rather small stature, with thinning white hair and a serene countenance. His experience in treating thousands of alcoholics had given him extraordinary insights into the nature of the illness. Alcoholism was, he said, an obsession of the mind combined with an allergy of the body—an illness of the body, mind, and spirit. Once the alcoholic took one drink, it set up a compulsion that condemned him to end up institutionalized or dead. After Bill recovered, Dr. Silkworth discussed this medical theory of alcoholism with him many times; and Bill in turn carried this idea with him to Akron, where it caught fire with Dr. Bob. It became a part of the message that they carried to other alcoholics thereafter.

When Bill wrote the Big Book, he invited Dr. Silkworth to contribute "The Doctor's Opinion." It is a remarkable document that holds up today as well as it did the day it was written a half-century ago. It reads in part:

> The action of alcohol on these chronic alcoholics is a manifestation of an allergy; that the phenomenon of craving is limited to this class and never occurs in the average temperate drinker. These allergic types can never safely use alcohol in any form at all.
>
> Once they have lost control,
>
> their ideas must be grounded in a power greater than themselves, if they are to recreate their lives. . . .
>
> Men and women drink essentially because they like the effect produced by alcohol. The sensation is so elusive that, while they admit it is injurious, they cannot after a time differentiate the true from the false. To them, their alcoholic life seems the only normal one. They are restless, irritable and discontented, unless they can again experience the sense of ease and comfort which comes at once by taking a few drinks—drinks which they see others taking with impunity. After they have succumbed to the desire again, as so many do, and the phenomenon of craving develops, they pass through the well-known stages of a spree, emerging

remorseful, with a firm resolution not to drink again. This is repeated over and over, and unless this person can experience an entire psychic change there is very little hope of his recovery.

This disease concept of alcoholism is so widely accepted today, it is hard to believe that the words of Dr. Silkworth were the first time it had ever been articulated. "The little doctor who loved drunks," was Bill's affectionate description of William Silkworth, whom he never stopped acknowledging as a crucial influence on his total experience and thinking.

I alluded earlier to the critical role played by the Oxford Group—and particularly by their New York leader, Dr. Sam Shoemaker—in the creation of the AA program. The Oxford Group was started by Frank Buchman, whom Sam Shoemaker met in China in the early 1920s. They began as a campus movement, at Princeton in the United States and at Oxford in England—hence the name. It was described as a "First Century Christian Fellowship" in the beginning, and its adherents followed certain principles: self-surrender (preferably on their knees), conversion (or "changing" as they sometimes called it), honesty, restitution (to people they had harmed), witnessing and sharing, and daily practice.

With regard to self-surrender, Dr. Shoemaker suggested that although a person might want to do this privately, it was more helpful if he shared this moment with another person, preferably a friend who knew his needs, with whom he could be honest and open. This Bill incorporated into the Fifth Step. Dr. Sam also spoke of personal honesty and integrity as necessary ingredients in the surrender experience, involving assuming responsibility for others. When the person is "changed," he said the desire to be honest and open with others and with God follows. He also spoke eloquently about restitution, saying that to test the reality of one's conversion experience, it was necessary to seek out the people one had hurt—family, friends, business associates—to settle past wrongs where possible. (AA's Eighth and Ninth Steps) Two more important Oxford Group concepts: the need for fellowship to share one's changed behavior and beliefs in small groups; and the need to communicate and share deeply and freely their common experiences and problems in an environment where they spoke the same language.

Nowhere was Bill's gift for synthesis better shown than in his ability to select and restate many of these Oxford Group concepts in the form of a program designed to meet the special needs of the alcoholic—and which, as the program became better known, proved applicable and adaptable to those with other illnesses, so that today there is a universality about the AA program from which many different kinds of people can benefit.

It has fascinated me that although (according to Lois) Dr. Sam Shoemaker and Bill W. were not close personally in the early days of Bill's association with the Oxford Group, and although one might assume Bill's break with the Oxford Group would have caused an estrangement, the two men in the early 1940s continued a lifelong, deep respect for and association with one another that lasted until Sam's death in October 1963.

Several other early Oxford Groupers also continued to be great admirers of Bill. One of these was Irving Harris, an early Oxford Group leader in New York and the author of *Faith at Work*, a well-known book about the movement. In February 1980 his wife, Julie, Lois, and I went to Bermuda to visit this fine old gentleman for whom Lois and I had deep affection. He expressed some sadness over the decline of the Oxford Group (later renamed "Moral Rearmament"), but he was proud of the fact that Alcoholics Anonymous (which he regarded as an offshoot of the Oxford Group) had grown and spread to become one of the largest and most highly regarded movements in the world. He was always open in his admiration of Bill for this achievement.

Although we avoided bringing it up with Irving, the Oxford Group influenced Bill in another important way; namely, in showing him what not to do. Part of the decline of the Oxford Group movement can be attributed to Frank Buchman's losing his perspective and getting away from the simple principles of first-century Christianity. His leadership inflated his ego, so that he aspired to change the moral character of the world. He wooed public figures with money and fame and used their membership to attract others. Small meetings were deemphasized in favor of larger and larger public gatherings. Bill was smart enough to watch and learn and avoid these pitfalls for AA, and those of other similar movements attempting to help alcoholics over the previous century: the Washingtonians especially, and the Emanual and Jacoby movements, and the experience of Richard Peabody in the early part of the 1900s.

Another book that Bill valued and that apparently influenced him considerably was *This Believing World*, by Lewis Browne. Jim B., one of the first dozen members in New York and later founder of AA in Philadelphia, wrote: "From this book of comparative religion, I believe Bill attained a remarkable perception of possible future pitfalls from groups of our kind, for it clearly shows that the major failures of religions and cults in the past have been due to four things: too much organization, politics, money, or power." A copy of *This Believing World* in my father's library later awakened my own pursuit of spiritual faith, as I mentioned earlier. I left this copy in the archives when I retired.

Still another book that influenced Bill was de Toqueville's *Democracy in America*. Bill called Alcoholics Anonymous a pure democracy (because all power rests in the individual members, who are all equal), and a dictatorship ("because John Barleycorn is the ultimate authority.")

I mentioned previously two other influences on Bill's thinking about AA's structural concepts. One of these was St. Francis of Assisi. From him Bill got the ideas of corporate poverty, lack of personal authority in leadership, and having the least organization possible to carry the message. The second was the controversy caused by Mary Baker Eddy's failure to give proper credit to others for some of the ideas in her teaching. "AA should always give full credit to its several well-springs of inspiration," Bill declared. And indeed, Bill did just that—to the point of overdoing it. But he sincerely wanted to extend his gratitude to all for their interest and help, no matter how minimal.

From these and other sources, Bill developed and defined the AA fellowship's Concepts of no authoritative leadership, the sharing of leadership, the group conscience as the final authority, and the autonomy of each group, including as Bill so often expressed it, "the right to be wrong."

Bill's influences certainly included the outside friends whom he valued so highly—and who were the source of personal help to him. They are the subject of the next chapter.

12

Bill's Outside Friends

*B*ILL'S POSITION AS COFOUNDER of Alcoholics Anonymous and its de facto leader as long as he lived wasn't all a bed of roses. Many members regarded him with a kind of super-reverence that was entirely unrealistic. It naturally led him to have doubts and apprehensions about his relationship with the fellowship, and he often suffered anxiety about his ability to live up to their expectations. For the sake of his own sobriety and peace of mind, he had to maintain perspective in the face of adulation. On the other hand, when he failed to live up to expectations of the members, many didn't hesitate to express their disappointment, both in letters and in person. It was equally unrealistic to expect him to absorb this criticism without feeling hurt—which seldom showed, because he could be philosophical and realistic about criticism. He listened and learned from it.

It is not surprising then that in difficult situations, Bill often reached out to nonalcoholic friends with whom he was in close contact. Most of his AA life he enjoyed close friendships with outside people with whom he could share his deep concerns and whose strength and understanding he could draw upon, as he could rarely do with fellow AA members—especially if a problem concerned his leadership.

Mr. Hanford Twitchell, a nonalcoholic, well-known professional man in New York, knew Bill well in those Oxford Group days of 1935, and he often accompanied Bill to Towns Hospital and to Calvary Episcopal Mission, where Bill talked to alcoholics. He says Bill was authoritative, a natural leader, and always had a troop of fellows around him. At first he was alone and didn't seem especially a part of the Oxford Group meetings, but that soon changed because people would follow him. He was always more interested in talking to and associating with drunks at and after the Oxford Group meetings than in carrying the Oxford Group message as a team member. Mr. Twitchell says Bill thought he could apply the Oxford Group principles to his own alcoholism, believing that for the alcoholic to be helped it was necessary for him to gain some degree of spiritual belief if he didn't already have it, and that the one-to-one relationship, so strongly advocated by Frank Buchman, was especially applicable to alcoholics and important in getting a fellow to stay sober. He said that Bill wanted to be concerned with just the recovery of alcoholics in the Oxford Group, while the leaders of the Oxford Group wanted to save the world. This is where they differed.

Perhaps the most important of these friends and the one with whom he was most frequently in touch was Father Edward Dowling. Overestimating the role Father Ed played as Bill's spiritual sponsor is impossible. On a dismal, rainy night in 1940 when Bill and Lois were at their lowest ebb financially and AA was going through turmoil and growing pains, he appeared in Bill's life as if sent by a Higher Power. Not only did they talk far into the night at the first meeting in that little room at the old Twenty-Fourth Street Clubhouse, but Bill continued ever afterward to lean on this special friend for spiritual strength, comfort, and advice. Father Ed was a man of great warmth and good humor, whose compassionate ministry to alcoholics in St. Louis gave him a unique understanding of Bill's pain and problems.

Another outside source of help for Bill was Dr. Harry Tiebout. He and Bill enjoyed a long and close relationship, which benefited Bill on several levels. In his work with alcoholics, Dr. Tiebout was the first psychiatrist to recognize the effectiveness of AA, and his professional support was tremendously helpful in persuading other psychiatrists of its worth. Along with Dr. Kirby Collier, he was responsible for arranging for Bill to speak before two medical societies in the forties, which gave AA a big boost at the time. He also authored professional papers that from a psychiatric viewpoint analyzed why AA worked so well.

Bill had great admiration and respect for Harry and used him as a sounding board on which to bounce off his ideas. With a psychiatrist's objectivity and insight Harry recognized that the fellowship as a whole was less emotionally mature than Bill believed, and he helped prevent Bill from turning over his responsibility and authority to the groups before they were ready to accept it. As far back as 1950, Bill was proclaiming enthusiastically that "AA has come of age." And Harry cautioned, "Not yet."

Bill relied on Harry Tiebout as a friend and on Dr. Tiebout as a psychiatrist who might help him with his depression. In fact he went to Dr. Tiebout for therapy in 1944. He reported that the experience had helped him understand his problem and live within his limitations, though it didn't do much to relieve the depressive state.

Another doctor who was a good friend of Bill's was

E. M. Jellinek—"Bunky" to Bill and others who knew him well. Dr. Jellinek was world famous as the scientific and medical authority on alcoholism. He was a cofounder of the National Council on Alcoholism (NCA) and the founder of the Yale Center of Alcohol Studies, later moved to Rutgers. Author of *The Disease Concept of Alcoholism,* he did the basic research in this field. He developed the famous Jellinek Chart, the curve showing the progression of the illness and of the subsequent recovery. He and Bill had great admiration for each other; at Bunky's invitation, Bill spoke at the Yale Center. And when they encountered each other at alcoholism seminars or NCA affairs, they enjoyed reminiscing and joking together.

Dr. Harry Emerson Fosdick ended his review of the Big Book of AA by saying:

> Altogether the book has the accent of reality and is written with unusual intelligence and skill, humor, and modesty, mitigating what could easily have been a strident and harrowing tale.

But the reviewer for the *Journal of the American Medical Association* (JAMA) ended up his review by saying:

> The one valid thing in the book is the recognition of the seriousness of addiction to alcohol. Other than this, the book has no scientific merit or interest.

I believe it was this reviewer, a doctor, who some years later was discussing AA with Mr. Charles Towns, who told the doctor how he had been repaid all the sums of money he had lent the society. The doctor replied that since AA paid its debts, it must be successful.

As for Dr. Fosdick, he always remained a devoted friend of AA. In replying to a gift of *AA Comes of Age* from Bill he said:

You give me much more credit than I deserve: AA has done far more for me than I can ever do for it; but I'm glad I knew a good thing when I saw it!

When we think of Mr. John D. Rockefeller, Jr., we think primarily of his interest in AA in the late thirties and early forties. But the truth is, he did keep in touch and wrote many affecting notes to Bill and others over the years until his death. An example is from a 1949 letter:

How gratifying it must be to you to know how many people your organization has helped and is continuing to help. Your leadership throughout has been an inspiration.

On the occasion of Bill's thirty-fifth anniversary in 1969, Nelson Rockefeller sent him a telegram in which he spoke of his father's deep interest in the work AA was doing.

Two people who don't fit specifically into any of these categories but who nevertheless were much revered in Akron were T. Henry and Clarace Williams, the Oxford Group leaders there. In their home the early alcoholics met until late 1939, by which time there was no question that the alcoholics wanted and needed to meet entirely by themselves and to sever any formal affiliation with the Oxford Group. New York had done this in the fall of 1937, and Cleveland by action of Clarence S. had terminated its relationship in the early fall of 1939. So it fell to Dr. Bob to tell the Williamses the sad news of the withdrawal of the alcoholics from their midst. The Williams, more hurt than angry, couldn't quite understand why this separation had to occur but nevertheless never ceased to be devoted to the members of the fellowship, nor to Bill and Lois and Bob and Anne. I seem to remember that when T. Henry died, more AAs attended than anyone else.

In late 1943, Bill and Lois made an ambitious cross-country

trip including California, where they visited Bill's mother, Emily Strobel, in San Diego. Bill spoke to more than a thousand AAs in Los Angeles. In San Francisco, he saw the famous Clinton T. Duffy, warden of San Quentin prison, the first correction official in the country to permit the founding of an AA meeting inside the walls. Warden Duffy was another of those nonalcoholics whose friendship Bill valued.

After spending the Christmas holidays with Dr. Emily, Bill and Lois drove to Trabuco College, in the California desert. Trabuco had been founded by Gerald Heard, a British philosopher, anthropologist, metaphysician, radio commentator, and mystery novelist whom Dave D., a California AA member, had been anxious for Bill to meet. Bill and Gerald struck up an immediate friendship.

It was through Gerald Heard and Lucille Kahn and her husband, David, that Bill was introduced to Aldous Huxley, author of *Brave New World*, teacher, philosopher, and pioneer of new age consciousness. Again Bill and Huxley had an immediate rapport—of which both men were proud. Aldous called Bill "the greatest social architect of the century." They carried on a lively correspondence for nearly two decades. I remember seeing Huxley on one of his trips to New York in the later forties when he visited the General Service Office to see Bill. He was a tall, impressive-looking man, with a rather hunched-over figure. Both Huxley and Heard wrote articles for the *Grapevine*. Huxley's article entitled "Man and Reality" also appeared in the souvenir book *AA Today*, distributed at the 1960 International Convention in Long Beach. One of Huxley's books, *Doors of Perception*, was eagerly purchased by Bill, friends, and myself. When Huxley died in 1963, his widow wrote a long letter about his death to the family in England and sent a copy of her letter to Bill.

The bond that Bill, Dave D., Gerald Heard, and Aldous

Huxley all had in common was an interest in philosophical questions in general, and in mysticism and psychic phenomena in particular. Heard and Huxley were close friends of David and Lucille Kahn, and Bill met frequently with them when they were in New York at the Kahns' apartment on Central Park South. The Kahns were longtime friends and supporters of Edgar Cayce, the famous psychic.

Lucille Kahn still lives in New York on Central Park South. I visited her again recently. A widow now, in her middle eighties she looked about sixty—a small, petite, handsome lady, sure of herself and articulate. She shared again her memories of Bill and the meetings that took place, along with her husband David, who died several years ago, in their apartment when Heard and Huxley were in town.

Bill enjoyed his close friendships with Huxley, Heard, and Father Dowling—in fact, he had many friends of their intellectual stature. And this was helpful to him emotionally, apart from his own enjoyment of their company. He was able to share his deep concerns with these nonalcoholics. He could talk about his doubts, apprehensions even, about aspects of his relationship to the AA fellowship: frequent anxieties about his ability to live up to the expectations of most of the members (he often agonized over his role as cofounder, as leader), the sometimes super-reverence given to him—or, on the other hand, absorbing verbal or written disappointment if he didn't live up to expectations at every point. Both viewpoints were unrealistic, and he honestly felt it impossible to be accepted as just another member; a fellow human being, vulnerable, imperfect like themselves. He thought long and hard about the role of leadership, which was reflected in his writing later on. These outside people, detached and removed from an emotional contest, were good for him, counseled him, advised often different points of view as perhaps AA members could not.

Nell Wing, 1970s, as AA archivist, at her New York office.

13

Archivist for AA

During my last ten years at the General Service Office, I served as the archivist for Alcoholics Anonymous. In many ways, this was one of the richest and most fulfilling periods of my life. The activity required some creativity and independent action, and an overview of AA history was necessary. So was a measure of persistence! My familiarity, in many cases friendship, with early members—Bill, Lois, and other people who contributed to the beginnings and growth of the fellowship—made the position especially meaningful to me.

Actually, we began this archival activity in 1955. As related earlier, Bill had set up in 1954 a Writing and Research Team, as he called it, consisting of him, Ed B., and me. But because of Bill's bothersome depressions and his feeling that a major AA history we had contemplated was too much to do and that he might not be the one to undertake it anyway, the writing came to a standstill for the present, after completing the second edition of the Big Book. So Ed and I were left at 305 East Forty-Fifth Street. In anticipation of the full history, we had had a huge number of boxed files and records of the office brought out of storage downtown and stacked to the ceiling in a section

127

adjoining the shipping room. Bill admonished us, "Now, Nell and Ed, give what time you can to getting all this stuff in order. It's got to be preserved." (As far back as the late 1930s, he had made the same suggestion to Lois, and she had filed away letters, photos, magazine articles, newspaper clippings, her own correspondence, et cetera at Stepping Stones, which now have become the basis for a well-organized archive up there and at the Al-Anon office.)

Bill later indicated the reason for his intense interest in preserving archival records; namely, to ensure that "the basic facts of A A growth and development never can become distorted." By the midfifties, he realized that some of the old-timers were already distorting the facts. Also, as we know, Bill was visionary; he saw the sweep and scope of the fellowship he had cofounded and foresaw its significance as a social movement to be studied by future historians, scholars, and researchers. So in our tiny quarters outside the large shipping area at East Forty-Fifth Street, Ed and I began wading through old boxes of group and office records.

Ed B. was an amateur criminologist, an authority on criminal cases and famous trials, in ancient as well as modern times, about which he had written many books. Besides being recently sober when he joined us in late 1954, he had undergone a recent laryngectomy, so he could not speak. He communicated by writing notes or using hand signals. For lunch we often walked down to the Tudor Hotel restaurant on Forty-Second Street. Initially, the waiter, finding that Ed couldn't speak, thought he was deaf also (a common mistake). So he would repeat our order in a loud voice, speaking very slowly as if we were mentally deficient as well. This irritated Ed and me to no end, but we came to accept the things we could not change.

Ed had an uncle, Albert Bierstadt, who is remembered as

one of the famous "Hudson River Painters" of the nineteenth century and a prominent painter of the American "wild west" days, along with Fredric Remington. He had also been helpful to several governments, including Egypt, with their archeological digs at one time, and they had given him many objects from their tombs or sanctuaries. Ed inherited these from Uncle Albert along with some American Indian artifacts and some Roman objects found in digs in England. Ed in turn passed along several small statues and other memorabilia to me—I treasure this lovely collection and Ed's friendship deeply.

Ed and I worked comfortably together as we got into the job of sorting out and reviewing the old letter files, though I didn't do much myself, since I had other duties, as always. But I could see that Ed was consigning to the wastebasket about 90 percent of the correspondence as "not important" enough to preserve. I did argue that we ought to evaluate the letters and records from several points of view before discarding, but to no avail. So rather than protest too much, after Ed had left the office each afternoon I would rescue the discarded material from the wastebasket and put it all back in the folders until it could all be reviewed more precisely by me or someone else.

As it turned out, Ed did not remain too long with us—about a couple of years all told. He did some preliminary organizing of *AA Comes of Age*, until he left. Ed was also offered some editing research tasks for the *Grapevine*, but his rather authoritarian and critical manner irritated the *Grapevine* staff, and therefore no relationship was established. I didn't see much of Ed afterward, I'm ashamed to say. He moved several times, including a long period in upstate New York. Finally he returned to New York, where he died in the late sixties.

In the fifties, most people knew little about archival procedures; in fact, the word *archives* was not in general use except in connection with historical museums or public libraries and often was confused with library structure and purpose. Few businesses or corporations gave serious consideration to the preservation of their business records; most European countries were way ahead of us in this area.

When Bill assigned us this task, I looked for a book or books on the subject but found little, except one with some helpful information on indexing and cataloguing, most of which I was already familiar with from library work years ago. I also visited several places in the city that I thought would have archival setups but found little of benefit. At the New York Public Library, for example, they took me down to the bottom floor or cellar, where there were rows and rows of letter boxes full of material that they apparently considered of historic importance and needed to be preserved—but they also told me I would just have to devise my own system. It was the same elsewhere; I found little experience or advice I could use—just "do it yourself, and good luck."

One day I read of a new "records management" service located on Forty-Second Street. Thinking, "At last! Professional help is at hand!" I hurried over. Two or three men greeted me profusely. (I think I must have been one of their first prospects.) After I told them what I wanted to know the manager said that to come over and evaluate our needs would cost something like $90 a day; that if we decided to hire someone, it would be $150 a day. I gulped, thanked them, and quickly left—only I had to find my own way out!

From then on, I simply relied on my own library and indexing experience, my instincts, and my knowledge of AA. In this, as I mentioned before, Edith Klein, a professional librarian, was helpful when we started to get deeper into it a bit later. In the early seventies, I attended a course in archives at the National Archives in Washington, D.C., learning the difference for the first time between library and archival science. I was glad to find I had made mostly the right moves instinctively on organizing our material.

But long before we left East Forty-Fifth Street in 1970, I had started to accumulate and categorize a lot of the records: conference reports, the several kinds of newsletters, ours and the groups', group directories, *Grapevines*, books, magazine articles regarding A A, P.I. collection, material pertaining to conferences and international conferences, to name a few. We also had Bill's talks, memos, and correspondence, which I had already organized over several years, anyway.

In the late fifties, to the bottom of Bill's letters to early A A friends, I would add notes that said, "Save the history records of your group or area and your own letters because we're going to start an archives." One longtime friend asked me in a worried voice, "Nell, aren't you afraid you're creating a monster?" All I can say is that monster was a pretty slow-moving fellow. I don't recall any mad rush to break down barricades to rescue A A artifacts for posterity.

In fact, there wasn't a lot of enthusiasm for this effort from anyone during this period of the fifties and sixties. For example, I had collected and stored most all of Bill's dictation tapes in a special cabinet, including long memos to trustees on important issues, correspondence with well-known friends, early members, and the like—a priceless, irreplaceable record, because they preserved his own voice. When the office moved in 1970 from Forty-Fifth Street to 468 Park Avenue South, the cabinet containing all these tapes was cleaned out and the tapes must have been destroyed. I never saw them again nor did anyone else. I was and still am heartsick when I think about our loss. The problem was and is to educate people as to what should be preserved for the future. One time the general files at G.S.O. needed room on their shelves, so the general manager at the time, Bob P., authorized all group correspondence older than two years to be discarded. In the nick of time, I fussed about it, rescued the old group folders, and had them sent upstairs to me so I could review what ought to be kept—from my point of view, anyway.

One beloved and perceptive old-timer, however, did indeed understand the necessity of preserving the history and, most importantly, experience of AA: Tom S., one of the earliest members in Jacksonville, Florida, and a past trustee. On his visits to the office during the sixties, we could chat about the preservation job. He would ask me about Florida AA history, with which he was familiar and most concerned about preserving. That was natural, as he was the earliest member there. I told him that though I was making headway in a minimal way, I had many other duties around the office as well. I was literally working seven days a week, but I didn't complain to him about that, for I loved every hour of what I was doing.

One day in early 1972, after not seeing him for two or three years, since Bill's death, I had another nice chat with Tom about our favorite subject. About fifteen minutes after Tom had left, in dashed Bob H., the general manager, saying hurriedly, "Now, Nell, drop everything else you are doing and get right on the archives!" Like the good SPAR veteran I am, I saluted and answered, "Aye, aye, sir!" And that's the way I became "official" archivist. I learned soon afterward that Tom had gone directly to Bob after leaving my office, saying, "While Nell is still with us, we'd better get her going on those archives." I could only think I must have aged considerably in those two or three years since last seeing Tom.

Not long afterward, partly because of Tom S.'s great interest and partly because we loved him and enjoyed being in touch, we asked him to chair a subcommittee of early members out in the areas for the purpose of obtaining personal stories and memoirs from them, plus others they could recommend.

With the move to Park Avenue South, the archival records, together with a huge number of boxes of material not examined yet, were stored in the big room that Bill and I had shared as an office. After Bill died, the room was partitioned into two offices. I remained in one for a while, then moved across the corridor to a tiny inside cave of a room, with my files stacked so high around me, visitors didn't realize there was a body sitting at a desk behind that tower of boxes!

But it didn't stay that way too long. I reported to Bob's administrative assistant, Midge M. With her enthusiastic help, the following year, 1972, archives was given its own space on the newly leased eighth floor of 468 Park Avenue South. My desk was in a large, sunny corner room with pale blue walls and pumpkin-colored chairs. The floor was carpeted, and we had attractive lamps. This office was flanked on one side by a small workroom and on the other by a sizable storage room.

Besides having Edith Klein's professional assistance, I also acquired a much needed secretary and general assistant. She was an AA member named Harriet G., who became in time one of my closest friends. Harriet was a well-bred lady who had become an alcoholic and recovered in AA. Her husband, whom she had met in the fellowship, had died just a week after Bill W. Her AA sponsor knew some of the staffpeople at G.S.O. and, as Harriet had had Wall Street secretarial experience, she was referred to our office for temporary work answering the influx of sympathy letters and cards arriving after Bill died. When this duty was finished, we engaged her for part-time work as my assistant. But since she lived alone and was absolutely devoted to the archives—and since everyone loved her and we enjoyed each other's company so much—she worked a lot of additional hours on special projects.

Harriet left because of illness in the late seventies, but we remained devoted friends and saw each other regularly until her death in May 1986. As she had no family, I was left to wind up her affairs. Many AA members and friends at G.S.O. still miss Harriet as I do.

Another assistant who is also a close friend still is Sheila T. Sheila is from a wealthy Greenwich, Connecticut, family. She made her social debut, graduated from Smith College summa cum laude, and settled down to be a society matron, married to a successful lawyer. Eventually they had four children. Somewhere along the way however, she became an alcoholic with all the serious personal and family problems that can accompany the disease. But with the help of AA and her own great spirit, she has overcome them. Sheila joined Harriet and me in the middle seventies. Though she didn't stay around as long as Harriet, I am still grateful for her time and contributions. We are good friends, and I admire her tremendously for her courage in adversity and her faithfulness to the program. We meet together frequently for lunch.

Harriet and Sheil were followed by a couple of other assistants and clerks over the years. Meanwhile, Frank M. had joined G.S.O. as administrative assistant. He was a tall, mustached man in his forties, rather intense. It turned out that among his admirable qualities, including a deep spirituality and a remarkable ability to share his AA experience passionately and articulately, was a great interest in AA history. On the organization chart, I reported to Frank as administrative assistant and secretary of our Trustees' Archives Committee; but in actual practice he simply took a closer and closer interest in the archives. Finally in 1982 he understudied me, preparing to take over as archivist when I retired.

But I'm getting ahead of my story. The year following my appointment as archivist, the General Service Board of AA created the Trustees' Archives Committee as a standing committee of the board; the committee held its first meeting October 24,

1973. There were three members initially; George G., chair, a college professor of communications who has made telling and lasting contributions to our department and still does, as a valued consultant and advisor; the Reverend Lee Belford; and Dr. Milton Maxwell, who also served as chair. He was a long-contributing, nonalcoholic trustee who later became Chair of the Board of Trustees. (He died in October 1988.) Midge M., who helped us so much, served as secretary of the committee, and I was also present, of course. Later, when Midge left, Frank M. took her place. At that first meeting, the main purpose of the committee was clearly stated: "To keep the record straight so that myth does not predominate over fact as to historical accuracy."

We developed our own budget requirements for office furniture, a card catalogue, framing of historic pictures and documents, display cases, visual equipment, tape and recording equipment, and other necessities. The committee also considered questions of policy. We defined our aims and objects, including classifications of the material and who may have access to the different classifications. They encouraged formation of area archives, granted permission to reprint from uncopyrighted archival material, and so on. The Trustees' Archives Committee has continued to meet on at least a quarterly basis ever since; the size has increased from three members to eight.

My first project as archivist, which occupied the entire summer of 1972, was to categorize and integrate copies and originals of Bill's correspondence files I maintained at Bedford Hills with those I maintained at G.S.O. Correspondence between Dr. Bob and Bill is included in this category, as is information and activities of Dr. Bob's wife, Anne, and Lois too, of course. (AA visitors to the archives tell me it is an eerie experience to hold in their hands and to read letters from Bill to Dr. Bob and vice versa in their own handwriting.) Later, Lois contributed valuable items from her own files: a duplicate of an early scrapbook, copies of letters between her and Bill when he was in Akron in 1935, and copies of her own diaries dating from 1937 through 1954 containing intimate and affecting glimpses of events and her reactions to them during those early and struggling years in their personal and AA lives. (Al-Anon has also maintained for several years, guided from the beginning by Margaret O'B., an attractive housing and collection of their fellowship's historical documents. Fran H. has also organized a similar archival collection at Stepping Stones.)

A second category of archival material besides Bill and Bob's letters and records is the history of the groups that started in the first fifteen years of AA, how they got started, and how they grew in different parts of the United States and Canada, and early beginnings overseas. The plan was that additional such records would be added every two or three years, as "weeding out" took place in the regular file department.

The third broad category consists of the business and financial records and history of the old Alcoholic Foundation, Works Publishing, Inc., and General Service Office.

Still another category covers photographs, displays, maps, awards, citations, art, large scrapbooks, and so on. Copies of the AA *Grapevine* and records from its start are also included. There is so much more—you'll have to visit yourself.

Most of the important material was microfilmed by the middle of the seventies and the microfilms coded, labeled, and indexed for easy retrieval. At the same time, we also undertook to record on audiocassette tapes the significant talks that we had accumulated on wire recordings, phonograph records, and other obsolete recording formats. All microfilms and cassettes were done in duplicate, with the second copy stored in a safe storage vault in New Jersey. I believe there are present plans to update the preservation techniques and prepare for computerization of information.

Special treasures are oral histories, personal and area history from old-time members, and area and state histories in written form. Collecting these is an ongoing activity, but I am so grateful we have preserved the memories of many members who have passed on in recent years.

I want to emphasize again that the archives is not a library. While the visitor today will indeed see bookcases (containing one copy of every printing of the Big Book and subsequent books) and a large "library" room with bookshelves containing books on alcoholism and books either mentioning AA or written by AA members, the visitor will also see an array of pictures on the wall and a variety of memorabilia and historical artifacts. One wall is covered with photos of Bill and Lois and early AA scenes in New York; another with photos of Dr. Bob and Anne, Sister Ignatia, and AA locations in Akron. A third wall is crowded with photos from all the international conventions since 1955. The visitor will see the Lasker Award, Dr. Carl Jung's famous letter to Bill, bronze busts of Bill and Bob made by an AA member, and other "museum" objects.

Two attractions in the archives are rivals as the all-time favorites with visitors. One is the carefully preserved first copy of the first printing of the first edition of the Big Book. A slightly oversize volume with a red-colored cloth binding, it is a gift from the widow of Jim B., one of the first ten members of AA and the founder of AA in Philadelphia (even before it was called AA). Jim B. is the person credited with changing the Twelve Steps to include the phrase (and the concept) of "God as we understood Him." The book bears a handwritten notation by Jim B. as to its authenticity and the signatures of scores of early members.

Recently, the archives has also acquired another wonderful treasure: a Big Book from the first printing autographed from Bill to Lois in 1939. Lois added a message to Todd (Dr. Bob's grandson) and sent it to him. Todd's father has now forwarded this book to the G.S.O. archives—a memorable and generous gift indeed.

The other prime attraction are the fifteen large scrapbooks of early newspaper clippings about AA. Newsprint deteriorates and crumbles to pieces over the years, so the original scrapbooks from the early years were in dreadful shape. We sent them to a really first-rate restoration firm in New York, who did an extremely laborious but amazing job. It involved soaking the clippings to deacidify them; then carefully drying them and remounting them on acid-free paper. Each page is then encapsulated in Mylar before the pages are rebound in durable covers, in chronological order. It is an expensive procedure, but well worth it because the finished scrapbooks not only provide a unique picture of AA growth from 1939 on, but they also show how the public regarded alcoholism and how newspaper writers reported on the new society. The language they used is amusing today; for example, one headline reads, "AA's Battle Demon Rum." With the changing attitude toward alcoholism over the years, the reporters abandoned the nineteenth-century expressions describing drunkenness and began to report stories about AA with more accuracy and understanding.

For example, our 1939–42 scrapbook carries headlines like: "Rockefeller Dines Toss-Pots," or "Secretly Helps Chronic Drunks" or "Bared as Angel of Reform Project." Another: "Former Topers Plan to Aid New Crop." Later on, this example of a good headline: "Alcoholics Anonymous—Costs Nothing to Belong, but Fortunes to Join." Give that one a little thought, if you will. The editors loved the term "water wagon," as in: "Life on the Water Wagon Extolled" or referring to Bill, "Water Wagon Head Visits Here."

The devices used to protect anonymity at the media level in those days bring a laugh today. One full-page newspaper photo shows a man wearing a Halloween mask, and there are several other pictures of whole groups wearing masks, like multiple Lone Rangers. Also a couple of guys wearing masks on their way to an AA meeting walking down a dark alley. (See Appendix A: Anonymity.)

Soon after the archives was established in New York, areas and localities began setting up local archives of their own—which we encouraged and fostered from the very beginning as an important corollary to our own efforts at G.S.O. Some of the earlier areas in the United States that come to mind were Southern California, Florida, Washington State, Utah, Oklahoma, Chicago, Texas, Missouri, Arizona, and Washington, D.C. Early ones in Canada were Toronto, Quebec, and British Columbia. Today there are 180 archival centers in the United States and Canada and in many countries overseas. Periodically, we distribute a newsletter called *Markings,* started in 1980 at the good sharing session after the archives workshop at the New Orleans International Convention to share helpful, up-to-date information among these archives in the field.

We have also explored ways of sharing our treasures with them—and with the rest of the fellowship as well. We have available, for example, a copy of the original prepublication draft manuscript of the Big Book, sometimes called the "multilith" copy. We offer a full-size copy of the 1939–42 scrapbook. Tapes of important talks by the cofounders can be purchased. Sets of prints of historic photos are available for framing. And so on. Probably the most effective tool we have for "taking the Archives to the Fellowship" is the filmstrip "Markings on a Journey," prepared at the initiative of Mike R. when he was chair of the Trustees' Archives Committee around 1979. I must confess I wasn't much in favor of this idea originally, thinking more in terms of a good-looking brochure with lots of pictures to share. But now I think the filmstrip is wonderful. It isn't about the archives; rather, it tells the story of the first fifteen years of AA (with highlights of later history), employing the material in the archives. You hear Bill and Dr. Bob's voices and see such early nonalcoholic friends as Sister Ignatia, Father Dowling, Harry Tiebout, Bernard Smith, and others. I do hope there will be another *Markings* undertaken before too long showing what the archives rooms look like now.

The biographies of the two cofounders, published by AA— *Dr. Bob and the Good Old-Timers* and *Pass It On*—owe much to the archival material as well.

I must share with you one of our most embarrassing moments: The "official" ribbon-cutting ceremonies opening the archives were held on November 3, 1975, immediately following the meeting of the General Service Board so most of the trustees could be there, as well as a sizable crowd of other interested guests. Chair George G. presided, and Lois W., Dr. Jack Norris, and Tom S. all made brief remarks. (George G., who guided us so generously and enthusiastically, was generous enough to say, "I'll never again hear the words 'labor of love' without thinking of Nell." My reply would be that that remark describes him also, and others.) Lois and Tom S. did the honors in cutting a blue ribbon to symbolize the availability of the archives. The ceremony was photographed, but after the food and coffee were served, the assembled group had their laugh of the day: It was suddenly realized that we had totally forgotten to tape the historic ceremony for posterity.

In 1981 the physical location of the archives was again moved as part of a major refurbishing and expansion of G.S.O.

The present site is on the fifth floor of 468 Park Avenue South. There is a large central room devoted entirely to exhibits and memorabilia except for a receptionist/clerk's desk. A research workroom contains a conference table along with a library of books, the bound scrapbooks, and other material. The archivist and his assistant share another room, and off this space is a good-sized storeroom, where the area histories, tapes, and other memorabilia are filed.

The first archives workshop was held at the Forty-Fifth Anniversary International Convention in New Orleans. It was a thrill to see such a crowded room, with an enthusiastic audience at this early meeting. Five years later another archives workshop was one of the highlights of the Fiftieth Anniversary Convention in Montreal—a special treat was having Ruth Hock Crecelius as a speaker.

Meanwhile, soon after I became archivist I began receiving invitations to share some AA history at AA conferences, conventions, and other get-togethers in the United States, Canada, and Bristol, England. Although these talks were usually historical in nature, they were never exactly the same. Sometimes groups wanted to hear memories of Bill and Lois and stories about the early days; sometimes, more information about the archives themselves; still other times subjects like anonymity (See Appendix A) or humor in AA, or simply vignettes from "my life among the Anonymii." When I was a senior in college, I maneuvered around to avoid taking a public speaking course—and have regretted it many times since! However, I'm pleased and flattered that beloved AA friends have asked me to share all these years.

After turning over the reins in archives to Frank M., I retired from Alcoholics Anonymous at the end of 1982, at the age of sixty-five.

There are so many other things to say about the archives,

but no time or space. But I do want to stress the point that it's important now to preserve the history that is taking place today in AA, to preserve AA's experience and the experience of the several movements in and out of existence before AA came along. In twenty-five years, fifty years, this decade, as every decade, will be considered an era when AA history took place, when new groups started. New members arriving today will be considered the "trusted servants" of the future. The AA fellowship is one of the world's major sociohistorical movements. We owe it to future AA members as well as to historians, scholars, and researchers to maintain as complete a record as we can of this society at all times, so its message, meaning, and contributions not only to alcoholics but in other problem areas can be recalled and assessed for whatever future purpose, fully and accurately.

Above all, I feel as other members do—even more as time passes—that it is tremendously important to preserve the AA experience so it can be useful to future decades of members and groups. History is the record of dates and events, happenings in time. Experience is what has been learned from these happenings, the meaning, substance and evaluation of these events. As far as AA's continuing stability into the future, preserving, evaluating, and being aware of its past experience is necessary.

14

Epilogue: What AA Means to Me

I HAVE ALWAYS FELT A tremendous sense of gratitude for my long association with Alcoholics Anonymous. It's interesting, in retrospect, how quickly I developed a close relationship to this beloved fellowship. I bonded early to it mentally and emotionally, forgetting about Mexico and sculpture and the anticipated freedom to flow as I desired wherever and whenever inspiration took me!

I'm deeply grateful for having had the opportunity to observe up close how the AA and Al-Anon programs work and to view over the past years, through a unique and exciting window upon the world of AA, the amazing growth, development, and stability of the AA fellowship. From a sociohistorical point of view it has been thrilling to see how the victims of other illnesses and behavior problems have successfully adapted the Twelve Steps to bring about their own recovery. The success of the widespread and multiple self-help movements that we take for granted today sprang directly from the experience and program of Alcoholics Anonymous. (It will be interesting to observe how the present trend to involve AA group participation as part of the whole addiction scene will affect "traditional" AA in the future.)

From my vantage point, I have watched the emergence in the fifties, development through the sixties, and explosive growth since the early seventies of alcoholism agencies and treatment centers. When AA began, no general hospitals, as far as I remember, admitted alcoholics under that diagnosis: there was only the isolated "drunk farm" or private hospital like Towns Hospital in New York, or a little later, in the middle forties, a floor or ward, as in Knickerbocker Hospital, also in New York, a ward brought about through the sponsorship and efforts of local AA members.

One of Bill's early visions for his as-yet nameless movement was to have a chain of hospitals for alcoholics. This grandiose hope was dashed when, under the direct influence of John D. Rockefeller, Jr., it was decided that "money would ruin AA." (But then the early members themselves didn't rally to the hospital idea, anyway.) I find it ironic that Bill was actually so far-sighted in this area. Today there are several thousand alcoholic rehabilitation facilities across the United States and Canada and elsewhere in the world as he dreamed there would be—except they are not under AA auspices. Yet AA is an essential part of the therapy in most of them and many or maybe most of their patients eventually end up in AA.

This phenomenon resulted in part from a change in attitude by professionals and the general public toward alcoholism, brought about largely by the success and acceptance of AA. Gradually the misconception of alcoholism being purely a moral issue and a behavioral problem has given way to recognition that it is a treatable disease. In fact, most professionals now subscribe to the holistic interpretation embraced by AA from its beginning that it is a disease or illness of the mind, body, and spirit, which was Dr. Silkworth's opinion.

The universality of AA's Twelve Step program is simply stunning. It has crossed barriers of geography, race, religion, politics, and time. Even as I write nearly sixty years after it began, it is still spreading. It has been a revelation to behold how alcoholics who are culturally diverse—from young people on the streets of Los Angeles to Confucianists in Nepal—ask for AA help, receive the same healing recovery by diligently practicing the same program, and eventually develop nearly identical structural frameworks based on sharing, love, and service as I also learned in attending meetings in Scotland, Ireland, England, Switzerland, Italy, and Israel over the years.

Ever since my days as receptionist at the AA office (we called it "headquarters" in those days), I have been agreeably surprised at how many so-called normal people (if there is such a classification; an AA friend likes to define the word *normal* as "a setting on the washing machine") desire to use the AA program. Visitors often stopped by the office to ask for a copy of the Steps so they could apply them to their own lives. A few years ago, worried about a heart murmur (nothing serious) I was being examined by a young female medical doctor. She asked me what I did, and I told her that though a nonalcoholic, I had worked for AA. Her face brightened up and she declared, "Oh, I follow the Twelve Steps. I'm not an alcoholic either, but I use and recommend the Steps too." I knew exactly where she was coming from. The AA way of life changed me dramatically. (I would not, however, expect to be accepted as a member of an AA group, because I'm not an alcoholic. An "owlcoholic," maybe, because I'm a compulsive collector of owls.)

I remained into my late twenties a "late-bloomer" type, emotionally immature, still retaining unrealistic fantasies and expectations about what life would hand me—often not too reluctant to follow its beckoning finger. But once securely enfolded by AA friends and philosophy, I began to learn by degrees to apply AA principles to daily decisions, to face reality; that is, to accept challenges squarely and honestly (most of the time, anyway), to evaluate events as well as occasional personal conflicts in my life with better judgment and consideration than before, with some degree of courage and humility, instead of running away or avoiding them, as I would do before. Also, I have learned to cope with unforeseen physical realities such as cancer, and accepting, gracefully I hope, the "aging seventies," all too often bringing losses of dear and close friends.

In many instances I too have been able to pass this way of life on to others. And that brings an added dimension of joy.

Today there are so many members of Alcoholics Anonymous and Al-Anon (not to mention the other Twelve Step programs), along with their relatives and friends who are touched by their lives, that I feel AA is changing the world! When I said that to Bill years ago he replied, "You can say that!"—meaning that he could not, for he could not afford to build up his own ego in that way, and he repeatedly cautioned the fellowship about such grandiose thinking. (You know, living your life one day at a time makes a lot of sense.)

Of course, I'm not alone among nonalcoholics who feel this way about the AA way of life. I've heard Michael Alexander say that just by being associated with the fellowship, "you grow and mature." And Dr. Jack Norris said, "We are all selfish and irritable and resentful at times. But AA shows us how to get rid of these defects of character that run our relationships."

That reminds me of my own concept of spirituality: namely, it is to be discovered in our relationships, in our being connected with other people and in holding onto faith. My favorite definition is credited to William Ward, who said, "Faith is knowing there is an ocean because you have seen a brook."

As a child I attended the Free Methodist church in our

small town—the only church there was in West Kendall. It was evangelistic, what today would be termed "fundamentalist." For our young minds, God was an old man, dressed in long white robes, long gray hair and beard, and always poking a long finger out of the clouds and condemning us angrily to hell for some infraction, or taking us to heaven if we had said our prayers that morning!

With that background, I realized as I grew older that I am not necessarily Religious—with a capital *R*. Over the years, I've tried to be open to other approaches to spiritual faith. In the sixties, for example, I read of Alan Watts and Dr. D. T. Suzuki and during that period participated in an early sort of "encounter group" in Big Sur, California, with a close AA friend. We broke up into randomly selected pairs who didn't know each other. The object was to try to form a rapport with the other person without talking at all. And we found it was not only possible, but a deeply enriching experience. I've always remembered it. At another time, I attended the Unitarian church; the minister was interested in AA (an AA group met in the social room downstairs), and he often incorporated some of the AA principles in his sermons.

I also attended Buddhist meetings during my first years in New York, which led me to explore more deeply my long-held interest in Buddhism. I came to believe that their tenets and philosophy were closest to mine. One of their principles is that each human being is responsible for the consequences of his or her own thoughts, words, and deeds, for facing these responsibilities with honesty. In other words you cause your suffering. The state of enlightenment that Buddhists try to achieve is one in which our inner selfishness and self-centered ego (which, when wrongly used, causes most of our suffering) are purged away. That's similar to one of the principal aims of AA's Twelve Steps. Buddhism connects well with the fellowship in many other ways. Buddhists believe that all creation goes forward, always changing and flowing, but always progressing, and we try not to resist this flow but to go along with it. They stress the need for inward concentration and meditation to seek the reality within that reflects the ultimate reality. Buddhism has no savior, no authority figures. It is a way of life like AA. Gautama (Buddha) did not want to be revered. He stressed the need for communication, for sharing. I don't mean to proselytize here (well, maybe a little!), but rather to share a bit of my own effort to grow and widen my horizons spiritually. This is another thing Buddhism and AA have in common: Neither of them proselytizes, but respects all faiths and philosophies.

From the beginning I was attracted to and caught by this special sense of communication and caring between the members of the fellowship. Not just a "caring for our fellow man," but their one-on-one caring, their loving each other without any thought of reward. This instant, unspoken communication with each other is unique; the "hug therapy" is a spontaneous reaching out—that's one reason people are drawn to AA. The other is that AA implements and promotes further growth after the alcoholic has quit drinking.

The principles of AA helped me when I realized I had to stop smoking. Watching Bill deteriorate steadily as his emphysema worsened, dying before our eyes, I made a decision (finally; it took four years) on January 1, 1969, and haven't smoked since. There was no way I wanted to die of emphysema; watching Bill go that way was painful. Like many other ex-smokers, I consider the smoking compulsion an illness too.

I also felt a special relationship to the fellowship because the male friends who were most important to me in my emotional life were in AA. And I'm grateful for their continuing attention and thoughtful caring.

As I've moved into my seventies, my whole life is rich and

wide, thanks to AA. I have wonderful friends throughout the country and indeed, around the world, with whom I am in touch and who continue to offer their affection and support. And I am so fortunate to have my beloved brother and sister in close and frequent contact.

I am especially grateful for the precious friendships of Bill and Lois and other beloved AA friends who have brought such meaning into my life.

Lois's passing from us in October 1988 was a devastating blow to all Al-Anon, AA members, and me. I anticipated the emotional loss but not the physical part; the exhaustion and depression that lasted several months. Not a day passes that I do not silently express my gratitude and love for her friendship, and to Bill for his friendship too.

I realize, however, that I am only one small example of what is happening on a tremendous scale every day; namely, that the fellowships of Alcoholics Anonymous and Al-Anon continue to bestow upon alcoholics, their families and friends, and other troubled people in need of spiritual guidance, their healing and ever-renewing benefactions.

Appendix A: Anonymity

[Speech given July 29, 1983, at Amherst, MA]

Good morning, dear friends.

First, let me express my gratitude for your invitation to share with you this weekend on the occasion of your twentieth state convention—it's a joyful opportunity to be reunited again with so many dear old friends and to meet new ones.

I think I'm retired. Truthfully, I haven't experienced retirement yet, I'm happy to say. But my umbilical cord to this beloved society is as strong as ever, and I feel it always will be.

Actually, I feel more than my AA extended family ties here. Ties to my own family background—Cape Cod and the Wings (that is, the non–Chinese and non–Indian ones)—go back to early Sandwich history. My family holds an annual reunion there each June.

Well now, the topic this morning is anonymity—and I must say I feel more than a bit humble, a nonalcoholic, standing up here, talking to you about this subject. It is a pretty large and complex theme.

I'm suddenly remembering the occasion, about ten years ago, when I had to fill in for Dr. Jack Norris on a Dick Cavett show. Dr. Jack couldn't make it, and I was sent hurriedly over to the studio—out onto the stage, a huge studio audience, bright hot lights, shook hands with the host, sat down, and the first question he shot at me was, "What do you mean by anonymity?" I went blank, stuttered briefly, mumbled something, and wished I was dead! I did get a chance to redeem myself later in the program, but I'll always remember the shock of that question. So I feel especially humble this morning!

But there is a lot of confusion about anonymity—that is, borderline areas in interpretation between what is public (outside AA) and what is personal (within AA). I'm not going to clarify any confusion, or get down to basics too much this morning, only attempt to share in a general way, some of the background, history, and experience relative to this important and unique Tradition.

Interestingly, many of our nonalcoholic friends have talked about or written about the spiritual aspects of anonymity—Dr. Milton Maxwell, historian, former chair of the General Service Board; Dr. Harry Tiebout, who often commented on anonymity's great protective value, especially to the newcomer. I especially liked the way Bernard Smith, another earlier nonalcoholic board chair, related its importance to the area of our service to each other. Bern said:

> The concept of anonymity today means to all of us the humility that comes with the willingness to serve without hope of gain or recognition or reward. If only all of human society could accept this concept of humility as we practice it in serving humanity—if only their willingness to serve was based on our concept of anonymity, instead of for reasons of pride or social distinction, how much richer would society become.

(To which—amen!)

And because of anonymity's importance in our society, AA

lives on in sharp contrast to other societies and individuals who failed in their attempt to help the alcoholic. For example:

The Washingtonian Society more than a century ago attracted a large membership in a relatively short time. Then members were persuaded by outside interests to promote or endorse their products or ideas, to take sides on political and temperance issues, to become professional or circuit speakers. In other words, they placed personal self-interest above the primary goal and spiritual interests of their society, and it quickly declined.

Individuals like Richard Peabody and William Seabrook, because of their alcoholism, also had deep insights into this problem and could articulate and communicate their personal interpretations in writing and counseling, but they failed to have a lasting effect.

The Oxford Group, initially a campus movement in this country that evolved into a semireligious fellowship in the 1920s and 1930s, did offer a way of life that helped some alcoholics temporarily, though the group was not aimed specifically at helping alcoholics.

But as success came to them, like the Washingtonians, it appeared that the old ego, power, and prestige characteristics surfaced, and the spiritual principles of the society seemed threatened and in danger of being overshadowed by the need to acquire more money and attract well-known names and their endorsement and participation. Interestingly, Frank Buchman, the founder, early in his work did appear to value anonymity, for he called himself for a while at least "Frank B."

Bill W. talked later about the Oxford Group and AA's early roots in the fellowship:

They had clearly shown us what to do. . . . We also learned from them what not to do, as far as alcoholics were concerned—too authoritarian, aggressive evangelism, absolute concepts which were frequently too much for drunks . . . dependence upon the use of prominent names . . . were mighty hazardous for us. . . . "Because of the stigma of alcoholism, most alcoholics wanted to be anonymous."

Let me just comment on that last aspect of anonymity.

Back in the beginning years, about 1936, 1937, before there was an Alcoholics Anonymous, there was as they called themselves just a "bunch of nameless drunks." Emerging bravely from underneath the protective mantle of the Oxford Group, they sought another protective mantle, that of being anonymous. Bill said of that time:

> Anonymity was not born of confidence; the bare hint of publicity shocked us . . . we were afraid of developing erratic public characters who . . . might get drunk in public and so destroy confidence in us.

There was also fear of being overwhelmed with requests for information, of more pleas for help than they could manage, there being too few members to cope, no office, no book or literature yet. So the necessity and practicality for remaining anonymous prevailed at the very outset.

It took several more years, well up into the 1940s in fact, as the membership increased and anonymity-breaking increased, before the deep spiritual and psychological significance of these Traditions became clear. It wasn't just something to keep the alcoholic from shame and stigma. Its deeper purpose was to keep egos from running after money or public fame at AA's expense. It meant personal and grave sacrifice for the benefit of all AA.

Experience proved to members and founders alike the necessity and value of adhering to this principle for more than its initial practical value. Bill freely confessed his own tentative feelings in the early days about his being a possible exception. Writing to an AA friend who had wondered if in a particular case he knew of, anonymity might be dropped, Bill replied:

> Just before publication of the book, I toyed with the idea of signing my name to it. I even thought of calling AA "the Wilson movement." Had I then dropped my anonymity, it is entirely possible that you and thousands of others might not be alive today. This movement would have gotten off to a false start entirely.

Of course, Bill soon abandoned any notion of his being an exception, and this instance is often cited as a first concrete example of the value of preserving anonymity.

Early in 1941, the question of anonymity arose unexpectedly in connection with the famous *Saturday Evening Post* piece on AA. The writing of the article had gone along nicely, members' names had been changed, everyone was pleased and excited about this major opportunity to let the public know about AA. Jack Alexander, the writer, had become a devoted fan. The article was all ready to go to press, when suddenly Bill and the small group in New York were notified that pictures would be taken to accompany the article.

Well, consternation set in at the tiny office and the *Saturday Evening Post* editors were informed that sorry, but no pictures could be allowed because of anonymity. The answer came right back saying in effect sorry, no pictures, no story.

So hastily a hard decision had to be made. Would the effect of the article upon the general public and especially upon suffering alcoholics, informing them about AA and the help available, justify the anonymity break? The decision was in the affirmative, and this was to be the first and only officially sanctioned breaking of anonymity by the AA office.

Over the next few years it became pretty evident that not everyone considered it really necessary to hide his or her personality inside or take second place to a principle!

Anonymity breaks began occurring regularly: Rollie H., a famous baseball player, and his AA membership made a lot of headlines in 1941, as did several other athletes. Even Bill, for a while in 1942 and 1943, thought that after all, certain people like him and Marty M. might do more good for the fellowship by shedding their anonymity. But again Bill realized the example he was setting and put the brakes on.

But not so lots of other members Bill remembered:

> Our anonymity dike continued to leak — AA members began to take us into politics, telling state legislative committees just what AA wanted in the way of rehabilitation . . . money and enlightened legislation . . . Some became lobbyists, sat on benches with court judges, advising which drunks should go to AA and which to jail . . . A liquor trade association proposed that a member take on an education job . . . Another was commissioned by a life insurance company to deliver a series of lectures on AA on the radio.

And so it went, threatening the basic foundation of the fellowship as members rationalized. They felt they were really helping to promote AA programs so everyone could see what good AA was doing! Shades of the Washingtonians! One had to wonder if AA had really absorbed the lessons that had engulfed that movement!

But that was only the beginning.

In late 1945 a movie, *The Lost Weekend*, had a terrific impact upon the public in that it portrayed the life of an alcoholic more realistically than had been done before.

Moreover, the movie seemed to open up a whole new perspective and interest in alcoholism; movie companies descended upon our small office—five in one year. We had lots of discussions—in the office and in communication with the AA countryside—on how much, or if at all, to cooperate. One contact with Hal Wallis of Paramount hung fire for about four years. A couple of scripts were offered while the debate continued; the project finally petered out in 1949 or 1950.

More than that, every day almost, AA was in the news connected to some facet of publicity—there were magazine articles galore. The same with newspapers—our clipping service poured in clippings at a great rate. AA was the subject of comedians and cartoonists, many being members themselves. There were new books with AA themes. There were documentaries and movies.

So perhaps in part, sparked by the whole atmosphere of good publicity coming to AA, several celebrities began dropping their anonymity, causing a lot of concern throughout the society: Theatrical stars, radio personalities, charismatic clergymen, among others, let it be known they had affiliated with AA and were proud of it.

Newspaper reporters, who over the years had always given AA wonderful coverage describing AA sympathetically, now became confused more and more as to whether or not they should print full names and pictures in articles. On one hand they had been cautioned by local offices and by our office about the importance of maintaining anonymity. Yet here were celebrities and other early members saying to heck with it. And of course the media and the general public were equally confused, as were most members.

So quite regularly we heard or read all about Lillian, a well-known entertainer, and her AA affiliation. The same with Norman, a well-known New York radio announcer, who finally wrote a book, at the end of which he was ready to announce again to the world how he had recovered in AA. A feisty, Midwestern priest, charming and articulate, traveled all over the country giving interviews. One was featured in *Look* magazine. He sold his books at meetings and blasted us pretty boldly when we kindly suggested he might like to rethink what he was doing!

These were only a few instances—there were plenty more. It was a confusing and stressful period, particularly if you worked in our office dealing with the public and all the personalities.

Of course, anonymity-breaking was a two-way street. Many members first heard of AA through Lillian. Traveling to Australia as an entertainer, she gave the small AA effort there in the middle forties an enormous boost. Norman was a most popular announcer and had a personal following. And Joe R. and his *Happiness Hour* on radio in the wee hours of the morning brought in maybe hundreds of members. No doubt about the good these members did in speaking out about their membership. But to quote one of Bill's favorite phrases, "The good is often the enemy of the best." Unfortunately this kind of anonymity break for personal purposes—often under the guise of doing good—proved the point feared early on: What if these members get drunk and the fact reflects back on AA in loss of confidence and effectiveness of the program? With alarm we watched this sort of break for the good of the movement growing! And slips did happen many times.

So the "celebrity syndrome" grew and grew. A member was heard to say to another, a newcomer: "There's a good meeting tonight—Mr. So-and-so is speaking. You know, the television comedian." Or a well-known member would receive a call from a program chair: "Would you speak at our anniversary meeting? I'm supposed to get a celebrity as a main speaker."

In 1944 the *Cleveland Central Bulletin* featured an article that said in part:

> As the years roll on and the miracles of AA are manifesting themselves everywhere, the question that is most difficult to answer is: "Where does the anonymous part come in?"
>
> Lately, our attention has been called to a most unfortunate habit that some members have perhaps unwittingly gotten themselves into. They have been citing the lurid details of some well-known members and mentioned their names, giving all the "juiciest" facts a liberal play, certainly to the detriment to that person's reputation. They argue that they are only citing facts, which is perhaps true, but after all, isn't it only fair that the individual be permitted to tell his own story when in his own judgment it will help some other individual? Stick to the fundamentals of AA in explaining the marvels of AA and let's not be gossipers.

A few years ago the English equivalent of our *Grapevine*, called *Newsletter*, did a wonderful spoof of this celebrity syndrome business, which the *Grapevine* reprinted in a 1972 issue. It goes like this:

> The year is 1995 and AA's entry into the publicity game is causing difficulties, as the television critic of a Sunday newspaper points out: "Wolfgang Snarle's comment last week on *Late Night Lineup* that 'Sobriety can be fun, but why can't it last?' may be causing AA's publicity men to think again. Snarle was referring to BBC's *Stay Sober with the Stars* and ITV's *Sobriety Show*, both with high ratings and both causing headaches to producers because of high casualty rates among the stars themselves. I learned that AA groups holding Meet a Star evenings are also running into similar problems. "We've no business in show business" in AA it seems!

Here's a look at the other side of this satirical coin. It is five years later in the *Newsletter* article:

Only twenty-nine members reached the convention at XJVK72 in October last. As number 543 pointed out from the chair, this was part of the price we must pay for total anonymity and it happened because the new code books had not been issued in time.

Number 187 of the CFMQP Group deplored the growing practice of allowing the use of first names at closed meetings, and foresaw the time when this relaxation of anonymity would creep into open meetings. It was the thin end of the wedge he said, reminding the convention that the letters AA stand no less for absolute anonymity than they do for Alcoholics Anonymous.

Asked by a member of the KKK Group whether something could be done about the approved pattern hoods worn by members at all meetings—the design makes smoking difficult—084 GSB said this matter was in hand, as was the question of marking all literature Top Secret—for the information of AA members only.

But let's consider seriously for a moment the meaning of that last news item from the year 2000 (God forbid it should come to pass!): Can we be too anonymous and with AA itself? A *Grapevine* contributor expressed two views:

Being too anonymous can mean failure to extend the helping hand when the opportunity arises. There's the story of a member who driving along, picked up a hitchhiker. The lad said he was on his way to see a friend who had a drinking problem and was worried about him. The driver asked him if he knew anything about AA, took him to a meeting. The lad took AA's message to his friend when he got back home. The driver later learned from him that his friend had joined AA and was now a new and happy person. In 1969 a study revealed that 55 percent of the thirteen thousand respondents came into AA through an AA member.

Again too, anonymous may mean failure to correct misconceptions of those who hold distorted views or have wrong information about AA. Again, the 1969 survey showed that the general public wasn't too sure what AA was all about. Only one-fourth questioned knew an AA member—the other three-quarters either held unattractive conceptions of AA or knew little factual information about it.

Altogether the survey showed that AA members are an important bridge to the fellowship, but that personal anonymity often prevents carrying the message on a private level. Yet many members still feel they are breaking anonymity if they reveal their membership to family, friends, doctors, ministers, or lawyers, for example—or even to G.S.O. (We receive letters from "Mary"—no last name or perhaps even an address—who wants information or literature sent quickly! Or a check may come in—unsigned. It happens!)

As Bill pointed out:

> In some sections of AA, anonymity is carried to the point of real absurdity. Members are on such a poor basis of communication that they don't even know each other's last names or where each lives. It's like the cell of an underground. . . . I think the long time trend is towards the middle of the road—which is probably where we should be.

And I think most of us would agree.

I can't leave this decade of the forties without mentioning how anonymity was preserved at the public level. In the filmstrip "Markings on the Journey," a photographer was taking Bill's picture, shooting into the audience—who sat with white hand-kerchiefs over their faces or their backs turned toward the camera.

So, let's now enter the decade of the fifties and beyond and consider briefly if indeed we have found that middle road to reasonableness concerning anonymity as Bill proposed long ago.

The decade of the fifties saw AA go in two main directions simultaneously. On one hand membership expanded rapidly in several overseas countries. Ethnic barriers and national boundaries were crossed easily in some countries, with more difficulty in others. Those countries where AA was well established followed the U.S. experience, setting up the same structural framework. This meant central offices, literature distribution centers, General Service Boards, and General Service Conferences. Nearly all benefited by our experience, and this made it easier for them to catch up and share together the same problems and progress at the level of the World Service Meetings.

On the other hand, here at home a different mood from the preceding turbulent years prevailed—there was a seriousness, maturity, and introspection. Bill's own personal growth and sense of leadership matured, and his dream of creating a General Service Conference was finally realized in 1951. Area delegates, most of them area founders, in those early years brought a lot of experience, a sense of responsibility, ideas, and creativity to each yearly session.

(Well, of course, it wasn't all serious: I seem to remember a lot of joking and high jinks about something called the "Thirteenth Step." That group elected a chair each year who at the end of the conference sessions, along with the awful singing quartets and Beatle imitations (complete with wigs), read his report. All I can say is that it sounded pretty hilarious, if highly exaggerated!)

The conference, becoming the voice and conscience of the fellowship, has been asked to consider all kinds of questions, a lot concerned with anonymity. It's been the subject of numerous workshops, panels, presentations, floor actions, and "Ask-It-Basket" sessions at all conferences, with the exception of two or three years. Here are some typical questions:

- What do you feel about having business cards printed reading *Alcoholics Anonymous* with the member's name, accompanied by a circle and triangle?
- Is it contrary to tradition to display pictures of the co-founders in meeting rooms, or pictures of other members still alive?
- A prospective juror was being questioned by the district attorney. The D.A. asked him if he was an AA member (there may have been members of the press there too). How should this have been answered?
- What about picture-taking at AA events?
- What is the experience regarding an AA clergy member breaking his anonymity at the public level?
- Is it a break of anonymity for me to tell the supervisor in my plant that I'm an AA member and would like to help with any employee alcoholic problem there?
- Are we violating the Twelve Traditions when in front of an AA group we say our first and last names? (By the way, the answer here is that the Twenty-first Conference recommended the use of first and last name with AA. All felt this would improve communications and be an aid to AA growth.)
- Should AA groups consent to tape recordings of AA meetings?
- Should tapes of AA meetings be offered or lent to groups or agencies outside AA?

· What do we do about anonymity when using sound and audiovisual cassette messages?

Questions also come from authors on how to preserve their anonymity when asked to appear at non-AA meetings, and about appearances on radio or television. At the archives we are often asked about preserving the anonymity of early members in oral history manuscripts and on tape. The majority of areas or archival centers prefer to use first name and last initial, the usual method. And that's fine, except there may be two Joe B.s or Mary C.s in the area, one of whom may not be an alcoholic or AA member but perhaps well known in the locality. It could be more than confusing.

Over its thirty-two years, the conference, as well as the General Service Office, has kept the non-AA public and AA informed about the anonymity Traditions via resolutions, annual reports and annual mailings to the media, and letters to the editor and to anonymity-breakers themselves.

There really does appear to be a more conservative, a more understanding, practical, and appreciative attitude toward these anonymity Traditions since 1950. Members do ask questions and seek advice. There are nowhere, it seems to me, as many breaks as there used to be. (There are always unintentional breaks of course, and misunderstandings or lack of understanding on the part of news reporters or new members.) Nor are as many famous names involved.

It's interesting that at the 1980 General Service Sharing Session, anonymity was discussed. The report said in part:

The subject concerns us all and puzzles many of us—it was pointed out that rather than argue fine points of interpretation, we should concentrate on using common sense and emphasize the importance of anonymity for AA strength—past, present, and future. Because of rotation among service workers in AA there is need for continuing discussion and education on anonymity.

I have the feeling I'm hearing Bill speak again; I think this kind of reasoning would meet with his enthusiastic approval and approach what he meant by seeking the middle road on anonymity.

I couldn't close without commenting on Bill's own maturity and growth respecting anonymity at all levels. In common with all humanity—saints included—he possessed an ego and would have enjoyed receiving one or two of the honors offered him over the years of his stewardship. But he always remembered those early days when he did think he could be an exception to his own admonition about the need for anonymity in AA. He faithfully avoided the limelight, and in those instances when he did venture cautiously into public situations (the Harold Hughes Senate Hearings on alcoholism, for example, in the late 1960s), he made sure his anonymity would be respected and protected.

Let me just give you a rundown of those awards that Bill personally declined or turned around toward AA itself for acceptance:

1. Discouraged any Nobel Prize possibility (late forties) by a well-known writer who wanted to propose his name. (I believe another writer had the same idea.)
2. Awards from colleges (given to the fellowship itself).
3. *Who's Who in America* (his mother declined this opportunity also).
4. Lasker Award (given to AA itself).
5. Yale degree (an LL.D).
6. A *Time* magazine cover story.

7. Posthumously, Lois declined a degree from his college of Norwich University, Vermont.

Bill answered many letters over the years concerning this business of receiving honors. He always shared freely his own experience and strong feeling about the importance of declining public recognition for one's service on behalf of AA. I think one of Bill's real gifts to AA was that he was able to communicate, not as an awesome leader, spiritually removed from a society of followers, but as he really and truly felt and thought of himself—as just another drunk. I have seen so many members over the years rush up to him, hug him tightly to his embarrassment, and tell him of their love and gratitude. He would immediately but affectionately turn aside their loving expressions and say, "Look, I'm just another drunk—pass it on." I can't tell you how many times I've heard him say that: Pass it on.

One wonders what would have been the outcome in other societies if those founders had adhered to the same spiritual principles as AA members—seeking genuine humility in all your affairs, placing principles before personalities, maintaining a one-to-one, or peer, relationship with the newcomer, sharing with each other, growing to maturity, and spiritual enlightenment. And how about the example of a leader who steps down from leadership—unheard of elsewhere?

Dr. Bob and Bill died and were buried without a lot of fanfare, though their anonymity was broken in the press, as was Anne's. Anne Smith died first in June 1949 and Bob in November 1950. So when Bill's time came the precedent was already set.

Appendix B:
Stalking the Wild Serenity Prayer

The actual origin of the Serenity Prayer has over the years been a tantalizing, elusive, and some still feel, unsolved mystery. It's intriguing to those of us at G.S.O. who have at one time or another attempted to trace the prayer to an authoritative, unimpeachable source.

The prayer entered unobtrusively into AA history in 1941. It was discovered in the "In Memoriam" obituary column of an early June edition of the *New York Herald Tribune*. The exact wording was:

> *. . . God grant me the serenity to accept*
> *things I cannot change, courage to change*
> *things I can, and wisdom to know the difference.*
> *Goodbye.*

Some fifteen years later, reminiscing about this event, Ruth Hock Crecelius, our first nonalcoholic secretary, said:

It is a fact that Jack C. appeared at the office [30 Vesey Street, Manhattan] one morning for a chat, during the course of which he showed me the obituary notice with the "Serenity Prayer." I was as much impressed with it as he was and asked him to leave it with me so that I could copy and use it in our letters to the groups and loners. . . . At this time, Bobbie B. [who became secretary when Ruth married in February 1942], who was also terrifically impressed with it, undoubtedly used it in her work with the many she contacted daily at the 24th Street Clubhouse. . . . Horace C. had the idea of printing it on cards and paid for the first printing.

All the local members including Bill W. felt its relevance immediately. As Bill said in *AA Comes of Age,* "Never had we seen so much A.A. in so few words." On June 12, 1941, Ruth wrote Henry S., a Washington, D.C., member and printer by profession, saying:

> One of the boys up here got a clipping from a local newspaper which is so very much to the point and so much to their liking, that they have asked me to find out from you what it would cost to set it upon a small card, something like a visiting card, which can be carried in a wallet. . . . Here it is. . . . Would appreciate it if you would let me know right away.

Henry answered back immediately and enthusiastically:

> Your cards are on the way and my congratulations to the man who discovered that in the paper. I can't recall any sentence that packs quite the wallop that that does and during the day have shown it to the AA's that dropped in and in each case have been asked for copies. I sent you 500 copies inasmuch as you didn't say how many you wanted. If you need any more, let me know. Incidentally, I am a heel only when I'm drunk, I hope, so naturally there could be no charge for anything of this nature.

For most of the 1940s called "the AA prayer" by members of the fellowship as well as others (by the late forties it became better known as the "Serenity Prayer"), this prayer has, as the *Grapevine* once noted, been credited to almost every theologian, philosopher, and saint known to humanity. The *Grapevine* also noted that popular opinion in AA (1950) favored St. Francis of Assisi as the author.

But there were numerous other candidates for the honor also. In *AA Comes of Age*, Bill said:

> No one can tell for sure who first wrote the Serenity Prayer. Some say it came from the early Greeks; others think it was from the pen of an anonymous English poet; still others claim it was written by an American Naval Officer; and Jack Alexander, who once researched the matter, attributes it to the Rev. Reinhold Niebuhr.

Indeed, the Greeks did at one time appear to have the edge in the author sweepstakes. Many AA correspondents frequently cited the Greek philosopher Aristotle, claiming they had read it somewhere or had been told that this was a fact. An example was Jim F., Maryland, who wrote in March 1957 that:

> D. McG., now in Chicago, wrote a lot of letters trying to trace the origin. I seem to recall that he once said it appeared in some form in ancient Greece I think, by Aristotle.

So too thought Paul K. H., a scholar and historian, who said he often contemplated writing a background history of the prayer. In a 1955 letter to Clem L., a Chicago newsman, he said:

> Four or five years ago, when I was thinking about that *Grapevine* article . . . I did some research on it. St. Thomas Aquinas said it in almost the same words and even the Greeks had a word for it—Aristotle or Sophocles . . .
>
> One point you mentioned is that the prayer seems to

spread so quickly. That's easily understood, I believe. First, it does fit each one of us. Secondly, if Chicago was like Washington in those early days, if an AA returned from a visit to another city, all the home AA's immediately besieged him with questions, "How many in the group there?" and "Do they do things the way we do?" and so on. Anyone coming back with that prayer, it would spread like wildfire.

In a letter to a member in the fall of 1948, staff member Ann M. summed up our thinking at that time:

> The origin of the prayer is somewhat obscure but the consensus of opinion seems to be that it was the product of the pen and brain of Aristotle. You can probably check on this at the public library but this seems to be the best we can do in identifying the author.

In fact, a few years later, Ann and I were chatting one day about the prayer and the difficulty in locating an author, so we decided to visit the New York Public Library, expecting to spend only a few hours there, locating once and for all the definitive source! We found a library assistant who listened to our inquiry, first with interest and then with increased impatience as we chattered on and on, enthusiastically reciting the background and various theories pertaining to the authorship of the prayer. Soon she stopped us and said quite firmly, "My dears, that will take a lifetime of reading and searching." We quietly walked back to the office, chastened and disappointed—and with some loss of faith in the whole library reference system!

Anyway, members all over the AA world continued to share with us what they believed to be possible origins:

Paddy M., from the Transvaal, South Africa, wrote us that "mention has been made that it goes as far back as Sanskrit writings." (Incidentally, both the popular "Yesterday . . . Today . . . Tomorrow" and "Look to this Day" have been credited to a Sanskrit source.)

The prayer was also believed by many people to be found in the writings of St. Augustine. In 1957, a letter-writer assured us that "the origin of the Serenity Prayer, or where I first found it, was in the *Confessions,* at the end of his life story." (Attempting to verify this source, I started reading the *Confessions* but have to confess I never finished—Augustine is very stimulating but difficult reading. Just searching carefully for mention only of the prayer or a version thereof was a tedious task! I've often intended to return to a more thorough examination, but have not yet!)

The writings of Baruch Spinoza, the saintly Dutch philosopher (1632–77), have also been suggested several times as a possible source.

Another correspondent said she had a notebook of favorite prayers that carried two Serenity Prayers; one attributed to St. Thomas Aquinas (1225–74) and the other to Reinhold Niebuhr (1892–1971).

Members also told us they or their children or friends had found the prayer in various books of prayer, of many different denominations: Episcopal and parochial schools and Protestant Sunday school classes. A member from West Virginia wrote us in early 1948:

> About six years ago, I was appointed to the committee of the Youngstown, Ohio, Group and in those days, the chairman opened the meeting with a prayer. Occasionally I would read one from the *Upper Room* [a small, daily devotional guide published bimonthly by the Methodist church in Nashville, Tennessee] but something was lacking in the necessary sincerity for the occasion. On leafing through my daughter's prayer

book, I ran across this one prayer, and it stood out from the rest. . . . I went to Neil K. and asked him if there would be any objection to using it since it came from a Catholic prayer book. . . . I used it Sunday after Sunday . . . and we asked a member who ran a newspaper to run off a few for us. That was the last we thought very much about it and never connected ourselves with possibly starting anything. This was in 1942. Now if you have something that will take it further back, I should like to hear about it.

One newspaper clipping came to us, attributed to the *Scottish Rite News,* no date, and carrying the headline "Ancient Prayer":

> This ancient prayer of unknown origin was found inscribed on the Chapel wall of the New Mexico Museum and Art Gallery, in Santa Fe, dating back to the 1600s. It may well be inscribed in the mind and heart of each and every one of us, especially in these trying times:
>
> *O Lord, grant me the serenity to accept the things I cannot change. The courage to change the things I can. And the wisdom to know the difference.*

One day in February 1961, I received a call from the New York Intergroup office, saying that a professor from Columbia University had dropped by the office to tell them that they might be interested in knowing that our prayer or something similar to it had been deciphered from hieroglyphics that appeared on an Egyptian obelisk!

I promptly addressed a letter to Dr. Eric Young, archeologist and authority on ancient Egypt at the Metropolitan Museum of Art in New York City, asking for his opinion and research help. He replied that he "had been cudgeling" his brains to think of an Egyptian source, so had his department, but noted that since there was no thesaurus or dictionary of quotations for Egyptians, it might take a lifetime of reading (What? not again!) to find anything like this. But he also thought the prayer rather alien to Egyptian modes of thought. He did not believe that Egyptian philosophy, or philosophers, could have conceived of human activities changing the order of the world and would have expressed ideas in much more concrete and particular terms.

It may have been Dr. Young who suggested that the philosophy of the Serenity Prayer was more akin to ancient Persian thinking than to Egyptian. Reading a little of the Persian poets and mystics, especially Abdullah Ansari, did indeed give a sense of kinship. A verse of another Persian poet struck me particularly: It spoke of the importance of maintaining a detachment or indifferent attitude toward life situations. Incidentally, it's interesting that many prayers—ancient supplications to deities, poems expressing deep spiritual values, or those evoking aspects of nature's beauty (I think of those lovely Japanese Haiku verses) often express or consist of three specific ideas, a natural trinity so to speak, as does the Serenity Prayer.

More possible sources came to our attention. In January 1961, Herschel G. of Maine shared an interesting experience with us:

> I went to Quebec to attend the exhibition that they always hold there over Labor Day. I stopped the first night at "the Old Fort Motel" about four or five miles east of Quebec. . . . Later, walking the dog, I noticed an old fort about 300 yards from the motel on the high back of the river, so I walked over to investigate.
>
> There I found a little fort, the last remaining one of three that had been built on this side of the river when they were preparing to defend Quebec years ago. This fort is in an

excellent state of repair, clean, neat, and well kept. When I came to the fort proper, I noticed that, where the casement window had been broken out over the door, it had been repaired with a panel, and on this panel was printed an AA slogan in French. I was startled and confused and thought I had translated wrong, but as I went along there were many other panels, including the Serenity Prayer in English and French, and there was no doubt in my mind that whoever caused these panels to be printed was AA.

I walked over to the little office and found a fellow, whose face still bore the signs of "pre-AA" living, and asked him point blank if he belonged to AA. He was reluctant to talk at first, but after a brief pause, he pulled himself up to his full five foot three and said, "Yes, I am"—he might have added "Wanna make something of it?"

In talking with him I learned that his friend Paul T. (in AA seven years) had acquired this old fort from the Canadian Government a few years ago, had repaired it, cleaned it up and made it available to the public at a small fee.

Another exciting possibility as source material showed up in the 1960s. In July 1954, the *Grapevine* received a clipping taken from the *Paris Herald Tribune,* an article written by the *Tribune's* special Koblenz, Germany, correspondent:

In a rather dreary hall of a converted hotel, overlooking the Rhine at Koblenz, framed by the flags of famous Prussian Regiments rescued from Tannenberg, is a memorial tablet inscribed with the following words:

God give me the detachment to accept those things
I cannot alter; the courage to alter those things which
I can alter; and the wisdom to distinguish the one from the other.

These words by Friedrich Oetinger, 1702–1782, an evangelical pietist of the eighteenth century, and the flags set the

tone of the School for Innere Führung (best translated as
moral leadership), of the Bundeswehr, where battalion and
company commanders and company sergeant majors are
trained in six to eight week courses in the principles of management and of the behavior of the soldier citizen in a democratic state.

This story, as you can imagine, created a lot of interest!
Here, at last, we thought, might actually be the original source
for the Serenity Prayer—back to the eighteenth century.
Whoopee! It sounded great! But, on closer examination, another story was revealed. And it's equally as interesting, since it
took a lot of time, patience, and persistence on the part of
Peter T. of Berlin to engage in deeper research. Here is a sum-
mary of his main points; shared with Beth K. of the G.S.O. in
1979:

> I have got together the most important date about the origin
> of the Serenity Prayer after a great deal of correspondence
> and reading.
>
> The first written form of it, as a thought, originates from
> A.M.T.S. Boetius [or Boethius, Roman philosopher and
> statesman, dates estimated A.D. 480–524] a Roman citizen in
> [the former] Yugoslavia, in his great writing *The Consolation
> of Philosophy*. He was sentenced to death before writing (pub-
> lishing) this book. Ever since, this thought has been in circu-
> lation, used most by those religious-like people who had to
> suffer. These were first of all the English, later the Prussian
> puritans (who met in New England and made it great!), then
> the Pietists (Presbyterians) from Southwest Germany (also
> emigrating to New England). Then the AA's, then by and
> through them, the West Germans after the Second World
> War.
>
> It was a professor (Dr. Theodor Wilhelm) from a North

German University (Kiel) who started to revive the German spiritual and intellectual life after the war and was responsible for the new education, especially in the new Germany army, as well as in higher schools and for nurses. He got this "little prayer" as thought and consolation from Canadian soldiers. He wrote a book (*Partnership*) published in 1953, and used this little prayer in it without mentioning any exact source for it. Very soon after that, this little "saying" appeared in all official places: in the rooms of high Army Offices as well as in the rooms of nurses and schools.

The trouble was this. This professor published his book under the pseudonym "Friedrich Oetinger." He used this pseudonym out of [admiration] for his southern German ancestors, where he himself originated from. Thus the AA's in Germany also used this name of Chr. Fr. Oetinger under the Serenity Prayer.

The second trouble was committed when carving this inscription at Koblenz. Sensing highly religious feelings in it, they surely looked for further information about the author ("Oetinger") in the Lexicon of Churches. Well, there is only one Fr. Oetinger, who lived between 1702 and 1782, a fantastic genius of his time, but was certainly never a serene person but rather a very resentful one, a mutineer and an alchemist besides being a high theologian and philosopher. He was a Pietist (i.e., not Catholic). He is one of the greatest spiritual or mental fathers in the history of German intellectual life. He lived in Swabia, where Dr. Reinhold Niebuhr might originate from. (The Swabians are known as great and zealous preachers!)

The third trouble has been the negligence of a special correspondent of the *Herald Tribune*. He saw the tablet at Koblenz. Where it exactly stood is not quite clear but it stands now in the memorial hall of the New German Army at Koblenz, where the "spiritual father" is Professor Dr. Theodor Wilhelm, pseudo "Fr. Oetinger." The tablet is quite a new one! This correspondent simply [accepted it at face value] without checking the name or mentioning the age of the tablet.

While this is a fascinating story in its own right and appears to correct a long-standing misconception, Boetius's connection with the prayer remains unclear and haunting! What were his thoughts and ideas that so affected succeeding generations of religious dissidents? And what was, and where is, the (circulated but apparently unpublished) *The Consolation of Philosophy*?

However, no study of the Serenity Prayer origin would be meaningful or valid without a review of the serious claim to authorship by Dr. Reinhold Niebuhr, a well-known theologian and for many years, Dean and Professor of Applied Christianity at the Union Theological Seminary in New York City.

Dr. Niebuhr's connection with the prayer came to our attention in the late 1940s. Henry S., the same Washington, D.C., printer who initially provided the office with the "God Grant Me" cards as they were often called, wrote to Ruth Hock Crecelius in December 1947, saying:

> One of our Group . . . says he has seen this prayer in Reinhold Niebuhr's writings as if it were original with him. I think I shall write him and see what he has to say and also require whether he knows how universal it has become with AAS.

Henry did do some research, checked with the Library of Congress, found that it as well as the *New York Times* book section attributed authorship to Niebuhr. Attempting to contact him early in 1948, Henry was told that Niebuhr was in Germany at the time.

In its January 1950 issue, the *Grapevine* carried an article on the prayer, entitled "The Serenity Prayer . . . Its Origin Is Traced . . ." Concerning Dr. Niebuhr it said:

It was actually written by Dr. Reinhold Niebuhr of the Union Theological Seminary, New York City, in about 1932 as the ending to a longer prayer. In 1934 the doctor's friend and neighbor, Dr. Howard Robbins, asked permission to use that part of the longer prayer in a compilation he was making at the time. It was published in [1934 or 1935] in Dr. Robbins' book of prayers.

Dr. Niebuhr says, "Of course, it may have been spooking around for years, even centuries, but I don't think so. I honestly do believe that I wrote it myself."

The article goes on to explain:

It appears monthly on the back cover of our magazine and every now and then someone tells us that we have quoted it incorrectly. We have. As it appears in the *AA Grapevine,* it reads:

God grant me the serenity
To accept things I cannot change,
Courage to change things I can,
And wisdom to know the difference.

Many tell us that it should read:

God grant me the serenity
To accept the things I cannot change,
The courage to change the things I can,
And the wisdom to know the difference.

The way it was originally written by Dr. Niebuhr is as follows:

God give me the serenity to accept things which cannot be changed;
Give me courage to change things which must be changed;
And the wisdom to distinguish one from the other.

Dr. Niebuhr doesn't seem to mind that his prayer is incorrectly quoted . . . a comma . . . a preposition . . . even several verbs. . . . The meaning and the message remain intact. "In fact," says the good doctor, "in some respects, I believe your way is better."

The *Grapevine* issued the magazine in a new, small format in September 1948, which was also the first issue to carry the Serenity Prayer. The September and October 1948 issues carried a slightly different version from the "original"—that is, *the* was inserted after *accept* and *change,* and before *wisdom.* Then for the next few years they reverted to the 1941 form. Starting with the December 1952 issue, another small change was made, dropping *the* before *wisdom.* The format has remained this way since that time.

G.S.O. has not included the prayer in its pamphlet literature except to quote it in historical context.

At least two other members (to our knowledge) early on contacted Dr. Niebuhr regarding the source. Gregory M., an author himself, wrote Bill W. in September 1951 that

a few weeks ago I wrote Dr. Niebuhr and asked if he was the author. His reply which recently reached me was, ". . . I did write that prayer. It was distributed by the YMVA to soldiers during the war."

Bill replied:

It is probable that the Serenity Prayer existed in some form or other prior to Dr. Niebuhr's authorship. Inquiries over many years seem to suggest this . . . now it is pretty certain that Dr. Niebuhr did write the prayer in its present form and we also have on file a letter from him to that effect. As a matter of fact, very wide-spread credit was given him in Jack

Alexander's last piece about Alcoholics Anonymous which came out [in 1950].

As a matter of curiosity it might be interesting to quote from the September 1950 Jack Alexander article. The reference to the Serenity Prayer comes at the end of the article:

Originally thought in Alcoholics Anonymous to have been written by St. Francis of Assisi, it turned out on recent research to have been the work of another eminent nonalcoholic: Dr. Reinhold Niebuhr, of Union Theological Seminary. Dr. Niebuhr was amused on being told of the use to which his prayer was being put. Asked if it was original with him, he said he thought it was, but added, "Of course, it may have been spooking around for centuries."

Alcoholics Anonymous seized upon it in 1940 [actually 1941], after it had been used as a quotation in the *New York Herald Tribune*. The fellowship was late in catching up with it; and it will probably spook around a good deal longer before the rest of the world catches up with it.

Jack C. (not the "finder" of the prayer), a newspaperman in New York City, wrote to Bill in October 1957. He said:

I, too, researched the prayer several years ago when I did an AA series for the News. . . . I called up Dr. Niebuhr. . . . He told me he had written the prayer as the "tag line" to a sermon he delivered on Practical Christianity. After church, a man who was to become prominent in the USO asked Niebuhr's permission to "borrow" the prayer for the USO. Later, when we got into the war, it was printed on cards and distributed to front-line solders only.

Bill replied:

I was very much delighted to receive your letter which carried such a splendid rundown on the origin of the Serenity Prayer. This question has always been in dispute and your answer seems more conclusive than any I have yet seen. We are running a research on AA designed to help the future historian who wants to do a detailed job, and you may be sure that your letter will be placed in the archives and labeled "important."

Another published article, source unidentified in answer to a question about the origin, answered by giving Dr. Niebuhr credit as the author, said it was first published in 1935 and quoted the prayer. Concluding, it said: "In addition to being distributed by the USO, the prayer was reprinted by the National Council of Churches and was adopted by Alcoholics Anonymous."

The March 22, 1959, issue of *This Week* magazine quoted the prayer and carried an editor's note at the bottom of the page:

This prayer was sent to us by a reader as a piece of wisdom generations old whose author was unknown. We recognized the prayer as an old friend, not nearly as old as our reader imagined. It was written by Dr. Reinhold Niebuhr. . . . The USO distributed it to American soldiers and the National Council of Churches printed it too. Later Alcoholics Anonymous adopted it. Gradually the mantle of age descended upon the words and people came to know them as centuries old. We tell the story now as proof that their message has put meaning into many lives.

Of recent date, two members from the New England area became especially interested in contributing information to the background of the prayer, describing the area where the Niebuhrs lived part of the year and sharing a letter from Mrs.

Niebuhr, printed in an undated issue of the Berkshire, Massachusetts, *Eagle.* Since the newspaper used the prayer, or it was used by other people in a political advertisement appearing in the *Eagle,* minus credit to an author, Mrs. Niebuhr reviewed the background for them:

> This prayer happened to have been written for use in the village church at Heath, a hill village some fifty miles or more north of here.
>
> The summertime residents of this village included many theological professors and even three Episcopal bishops. All in turn preached and took service in the village Congregational Church. My husband wrote out this prayer for such an occasion, and afterward a friend and neighbor, the late Howard Chandler Robbins, who formerly had been dean of the Cathedral of St. John the Divine in New York, asked him for a copy. My husband reached into his pocket and handed it over to Dr. Robbins. Dr. Robbins asked him if he might have it printed in a monthly bulletin which was issued by the Commission on Social Justice of the then Federal Council of Churches of which he, Dr. Robbins, was then chairman. This was in the early days of World War II.
>
> After this, the prayer had quite a history. The USO or some such organization asked for the use of it, and copies were printed, I believe, in the millions. Various personages—admirals, commanders, and others—used it and indeed often authorship was ascribed to them.
>
> At times, other organizations have asked for the use of it. An Episcopalian sisterhood in the Middle West printed it very nicely on little cards. Also Alcoholics Anonymous have used it widely with permission. When they use it, apparently, in their sessions or in their literature, they do not always give the author's name. Every so often however, in their periodicals, they would give the story of the prayer and its authorship.
>
> My husband used and preferred the following form:

"God, give us grace to accept with serenity the things that cannot be
   changed,
Courage to change the things which should be changed,
and the wisdom to distinguish the one from the other."

When in England last summer, I noted the prayer printed
on cards was on sale at most of the bookstores at the cathe-
drals and abbey churches. No authorship was given. So since
then, I have written to the cathedral chapters in the same
vein I am writing now.

The claim for authorship on behalf of Dr. Niebuhr is formi-
dable—no doubt about that at all. At the very least, he certainly
authored one version, of which the 1941 obituary prayer could
have been an adaptation.

And yet . . .

There is still another source to consider that also needs
more investigation. Back in the late 1950s a staff member,
Anita R., browsing in a downtown New York bookstore, came
upon a small card beautifully bordered with a scrolled design,
in which was centered a printed prayer that read:

A Prayer
Almighty God, our Heavenly Father,
Give us serenity to accept what cannot
be changed, Courage to change what
should be changed, and Wisdom to know
the one from the other; through Jesus
Christ, our Lord.
Amen
From a fourteenth-century prayer
often called the "General's Prayer"

The card originated at a bookshop in England, called Mobrays.
Since that time (1957) we've received at least two other

references to this particular version. The writer quoted from earlier in this letter (citing versions by St. Thomas Aquinas and Dr. Niebuhr) had further information to offer. She said:

> I then found the prayer in another book, *Between Dawn and Dark* by Frederick W. Kates and the prayer was marked "Fourteenth Century" and the words: "Almighty God, our heavenly Father, give us serenity to accept what cannot be changed, courage to change what should be changed and wisdom to know the one from the other."

She wondered: If this was a valid version, could it then be attributed to Dr. Niebuhr?

We also received some years ago a magazine article unidentified as to source and date but authored by Charles F. Kemp, First Christian Church, Lincoln, Nebraska. This excellent article, entitled "A Prayer for Serenity and Courage," begins:

> Some years ago, Russell Dicks, who was then Chaplain of Wesley Memorial Hospital in Chicago published a little book of meditations for the sick. (Dicks, *Comfort Ye My People,* Macmillan, 1947). In it he included a short, simple prayer, complete in one sentence that contains three ideas. . . . "O God, and heavenly Father, grant us the serenity of mind to accept that which cannot be changed, the courage to change that which can be changed, and the wisdom to tell the one from the other, through Jesus Christ our Lord."
>
> It isn't often that a prayer becomes widely quoted, but this one has been. I have seen it referred to in many different situations. Sometimes it is credited to different authors; often it is quoted anonymously. Not long ago I heard an address by a man who had been a medical missionary. He closed his address by saying something like this: "What is needed is the spirit of the prayer of Phillip Brooks, 'God grant us the serenity of mind to accept what cannot be changed, the courage to

change what can be changed, and the wisdom to tell the one from the other.' "

Mr. Kemp mentioned that AA also uses this same prayer. He continues:

The reason that this prayer has been referred to so widely has been because it is worded so simply and so clearly and because it speaks so specifically to man's needs.

There seems to remain a touch of mystery still, a lingering uncertainty about whose "pen and brain" first shaped these timeless thoughts.

In any case, for almost forty years now, the Serenity Prayer has become so deeply imbedded, so closely woven into the fabric, into the very tapestry of AA thinking, living, and philosophy that it's difficult to remember it did not originate within AA itself.

Bill W. said it clearly, many years ago, in thanking an AA friend for the plaque upon which the prayer was inscribed:

"In creating AA, the Serenity Prayer has been a most valuable building block—indeed, a cornerstone."

The thought has been expressed more than once: This prayer, whatever its ancient or modern origin, seems to have been born, at least in spirit, far back in time, out of an ancient perception and a suffering wisdom. Excepting for the Lord's Prayer and the Prayer of St. Francis, no other quotation or concept at once so practical and so spiritual has taken over the mind and heart of every member who begins the AA journey to sobriety and rebirth.

In conclusion, let me quote again from Paul K. H.:

With all due respect to Doctor Niebuhr, I have the distinct impression that the quotation, other words, perhaps, but the same thought, go way back. I'm sure Doctor Niebuhr would be the first to agree. He would probably say that any such prayer, or any verity, is, as we say of the AA program, "as old as eternity and as new as tomorrow."

There have been many variations of the prayer, besides the version found in the 1941 *New York Herald Tribune*. Here are a few we've collected over the years:

"God give me the composure
To accept the things I cannot change
The courage to change the things I can
And the wisdom to know the difference between the two."

"God grant us the serenity to accept that which
we cannot change,
Courage to change that which we can
and the wisdom to know the difference."

"Give me the serenity to accept what cannot be changed,
Give me the courage to change what can be changed,
The wisdom to know one from the other."

Chester Nimitz made an adaptation as follows:

"God grant me the courage to change the things I can change,
The serenity to accept those I cannot change,
And the wisdom to know the difference.
But, God grant me the courage not to give up on what I think is
right even though I think it is hopeless."

This version appeared, according to Jim F., a number of times in the Hagerstown, Maryland, *Almanac*. (The last reprint was in 1952.) The prayer is credited to Bishop Oliver J. Hart:

> *"God give us the fortitude to endure the things which cannot be changed, and the courage to change things which should be changed, and the wisdom to know one from the other."*

At the risk of appearing too frivolous, there have been some humorous yet apt endings to the prayer: Erma Bombeck, the popular writer, gave this version:

> *"God Grant me the serenity to accept the things I cannot change, courage to change the things I can, and the wisdom to keep my mouth shut when I don't know the difference."*

Someone else suggested this ending:

> *". . . and the wisdom to keep my mouth shut even when I know I'm right!"*

ABOUT THE AUTHOR

NELL WING was born in upstate New York, daughter of a judge/schoolteacher and a member of the Women's Christian Temperance Union. A series of "coincidences" brought her into service as secretary, aide, and friend to Bill W., a cofounder of AA. She was also a close friend and confidante of Lois W., cofounder of Al-Anon. This position in the family of Bill and Lois and as AA archivist have given her unique insights into the formation and growth of AA, along with perspectives on early AA members and "outside friends." Nell lives in New York City.

The author in 1990, displaying her fondness for drawings, as well as stuffed animals, of owls.

About Hazelden Publishing

As part of the Hazelden Betty Ford Foundation, Hazelden Publishing offers both cutting-edge educational resources and inspirational books. Our print and digital works help guide individuals in treatment and recovery, and their loved ones. Professionals who work to prevent and treat addiction also turn to Hazelden Publishing for evidence-based curricula, digital content solutions, and videos for use in schools, treatment programs, correctional programs, and electronic health records systems. We also offer training for implementation of our curricula.

Through published and digital works, Hazelden Publishing extends the reach of healing and hope to individuals, families, and communities affected by addiction and related issues.

For more information about Hazelden publications,
please call **800-328-9000**
or visit us online at **hazelden.org/bookstore**.